THE PONY CLUB: DREAM AND REALITY

THE PONY CLUB
Dream and Reality

MERIEL BUXTON

Foreword by Dawn Wofford

Chairman of the Pony Club

• THE •
SPORTSMAN'S
PRESS
LONDON

Published by The Sportsman's Press 1994

FOR ROSE AND HUGH
Without whom my acquaintance with the Pony Club might have
finished soon after my own C Test

A catalogue record for this book
is available from the British Library

ISBN 0–948253–70–3

Printed in Great Britain by
Redwood Books

CONTENTS

ACKNOWLEDGEMENTS

I would like to thank all the people who have so kindly helped me with this book, showing me how the Pony Club's success depends on the remarkable and dedicated people involved at every level: at Headquarters, as officials, instructors, parents and other helpers and as Members and Associates. I am particularly grateful to Mrs Dawn Wofford, Chairman of the Pony Club, for kindly writing a Foreword to this book and to Miss Catherine Moir, Executive Secretary of the Pony Club, for so promptly finding time to comment constructively on the text.

My especial thanks are due to all those Members and Associates who have been interviewed for this book, as well as to their families, for their co-operation, help and encouragement; to the District Commissioners, Branch Secretaries and Area Representatives who have put me in touch with them, and to officials who kindly offered their assistance but whose branches I was sadly unable to visit. I received particular hospitality and help from Mrs Sarita Perkins, and from Mrs S. Angell, Mrs J. Dixey, Mrs S. Gardner, Sister Mary Joy Langdon, Mr R. Noble, Mr Ross Nye, Mrs L.M. Patterson, Mrs J. Roe and Mrs M. Wyman, and help from Mrs L. Bloor, Mr Peter Brackett, Mrs C. Davies, Miss L. Greaves, Mrs P. Macneal, Mrs D. Sleight and Mrs A. Yeoman.

I would also like to thank *Horse and Hound* for permission to use the poem given at the end of the chapter on Parents.

I am most grateful too for the help I received in finding illustrations from Julia Allen, Peter Brackett, Gillian Berry, Brian Bucklar, Rita Buckley, Iain Burns, James and Hugh Buxton, Sue Eeley, Christopher Gardner, Carolyn Gerard, Linda Greaves, Max Hastings, Sister Mary Joy Langdon, Bob Langrish, Andrew McDowall, Jim Meads, Martin Pawson, Pleasure Prints (Crookham Common), D.H. Roberts, Sophie Roe, Paul Saville (Pleasure Prints), Daphne Sleight, A. & B. Sorohan, David Stephens and the *Tavistock Times Gazette*.

Finally, I would like to thank my husband James for all his encouragement, understanding, support and constructive criticism, Rose and Hugh for their patience and help throughout not only the writing of this book but their complete Pony Club careers (having a mother who is a District Commissioner is a major disadvantage) and Hugh for his invaluable assistance with the word processor.

NOTE: Ages when given are those of Members and Associates at the time when I interviewed them.

LIST OF PLATES

FOREWORD

Meriel Buxton has taken infinite trouble to produce a most detailed account of the Pony Club. She has painted an accurate and interesting picture of this unique voluntary youth organisation, which comes in many guises but never quite loses its objectives to teach horsemanship, sportsmanship, citizenship and loyalty.

The Pony Club's doors are always open – not only to new members but to the enormous amount of adult help needed to take on a miscellany of essential tasks. Depending on the nature of a Branch, these might range from cutting sandwiches for the picnic ride, to organising volley-ball in the evenings at camp. There is a place for every new member who wishes to take part and for every adult who will help.

I hope that, by explaining the characteristics of the Pony Club, the book will encourage those at present outside its scope to become involved. It will also serve as a useful historical record.

Undoubtedly, for past and present members and friends, this true labour of love will give great pleasure and will bring back many special memories of Pony Club life.

Dawn Wofford
Chairman of the Pony Club

Steps down at the Horse Trials Championships
at Weston Park 1991. *(Bob Langrish)*

INTRODUCTION

A DREAM OF PONIES

The Pony Club offers many children and teenagers the chance to realise their dreams. For some, the dreams are simply of spending long hours with a beloved pony, riding and caring for it. Some dream of camping with their friends, of games and jokes and water fights and fun. Some live in high-rise flats in the inner city, yet dream of riding a pony. Some dream of learning new skills, of passing tests, of acquiring qualifications which will one day enable them to earn a living from the sport they love. Some long to ride a dressage test with the smooth precision of a professional, or to feel the tension approaching the final fence clear in a jump-off. Many crave the excitement of riding cross-country, galloping on and surmounting the challenge of demanding obstacles. Some dream of the bright lights, the crowd, the thunderous applause and the thrill of the final of the Mounted Games Championship for the Prince Philip Cup at Wembley. For many others the dream is of long hot summer days exploring the countryside on picnic rides and mounted expeditions. Some yearn for competition in a range of sports, polo and polocrosse, of running, swimming and shooting in the tetrathlon. Some dream of one day sharing the pleasure they have had in horses by teaching others.

For others the dream is of visiting far-off lands, in exchanges with like-minded contemporaries across the world, as members of teams or perhaps through jobs with horses. Many dream of riding round Badminton, of Olympic glory: for a tiny handful even these dreams may one day come true. Others' interests may lie elsewhere in the world of the horse, on the race course, in the hunting field or in the showring: for these too there is no better gateway. Many more may simply seek an interest, for a year or for a lifetime. Some seek the excitement they might otherwise try to find in anti-social or dangerous behaviour. Others are in search of quieter ways and older values. Paradoxically the Pony Club offers both extremes.

Many of these dreams can become reality through the Pony Club. Even those aiming for glory far beyond its confines may find in it the springboard which eventually enables them to succeed. All should find kindred spirits with whom to share the experiences they seek. Whether or not the dreams are ultimately fulfilled, all should learn a little and have some fun along the way. In this book, many members will tell how their own dreams have developed. To understand them fully, we must first consider the basic structure of the organisation and how it works.

— 1 —

THE ORGANISATION

The Pony Club has almost 40,000 Members and Associates in the United Kingdom, divided between 366 branches. With more than 1,800 overseas branches, world wide membership exceeds 100,000. It is an enormous organisation, the largest of riders in the world, and yet through the branch structure every single member, and almost every pony, is personally known to those arranging activities for them.

For branches are, in the words of the *Yearbook* (the Pony Club's 'bible'), 'self-contained, self-governing and self-supporting'. They vary in size: there can be as many as 383 members in a branch or as few as eight, though perhaps a typical branch might be thought of as having around a hundred members. There is no minimum age for membership, though some branches are more enthusiastic than others in providing activities for very young, perhaps pre-school, children. Those over eighteen are known as Associates. Membership ceases at the end of the year in which an Associate becomes twenty-one.

Every branch is run by a District Commissioner and a local Committee, all of whom are volunteers. The District Commissioner has been described as a cross between a favourite great aunt or uncle and a headmaster or headmistress. He, or today more frequently she, is Chairman of the local Committee and takes overall responsibility for everything which happens in the branch. To make sure that the position is not abused, people with a financial interest in buying, selling or leasing horses, keeping a livery yard or teaching riding cannot become District Commissioners without special permission.

The Committee will include at least four members besides the District Commissioner. The Secretary in particular works extremely hard in the day-to-day management of the branch. Other officials are appointed to fulfill the needs of each individual branch. If there is a Chief Instructor, he or she will usually plan the rallies and tests so as to help each individual member to learn as much as possible through the Club.

With each making its own arrangements, branches develop different characteristics, allowing people, especially those close to the boundaries, to pick the branch with the approach closest to their own, though most join their local branch. Some branches encourage very young members, or are more competitive, or offer minority sports such as polo or polocrosse. Rules prevent members changing branches so as to be selected for particular teams, but their individuality allows families or members more choice.

But all branches in the United Kingdom are subject to the same overall control. Pony Club Headquarters, together with those of the British Horse Society, which is the parent organisation of the Pony Club, are based at Stoneleigh in Warwickshire. From these offices the Pony Club is administered by a small professional team headed by Lt Colonel T.W. Kopanski, who has been the Director since 1986. An exceptionally gifted instructor himself, his efficiency and charm have made him a most successful leader. He is ably assisted by Miss Catherine Moir, the Executive Secretary, who has held office since 1973. For many branch officials, ringing in with a question or request, she is the voice of Headquarters, calm, competent, completely unflappable and a mine of information on everything to do with the Pony Club. In 1990 Mr Peter Lord was appointed Development Officer and has now become a familiar face at Pony Club gatherings all over Britain. These three, with two assistants, are the only full-time employees. The Chairman of the Pony Club is Mrs Dawn Wofford, who puts in long hours on its behalf voluntarily, and who is the inspiration for many

Mrs Gill Painter takes a break from instructing at the Woodland Pytchley Camp to school her dog. *(A. & B. Sorohan: Event Prints)*

of the best ideas currently under discussion. She first achieved fame as the great Show Jumper Dawn Palethorpe.

The real decisions affecting the Pony Club nationally are taken by the Pony Club Council. All the branches in the United Kingdom are divided up into nineteen geographical Areas, identified by numbers. For example, twenty-four named branches in northern Scotland make up Area 1 and fourteen branches in Devon and Cornwall comprise Area 16. The District Commissioners in each Area elect an Area Representative, who may be a current District Commissioner, but is unlikely to be because of the volume of work involved. Each of these nineteen Area Representatives then serves on the Pony Club Council, together with up to 12 members appointed by the British Horse Society.

The grouping of branches into Areas is of vital importance for Pony Club competitions. Each Area arranges competitions between the branches of that Area (known as the Inter-Branch or Area competitions) in Horse Trials (or One Day Eventing), Showjumping, Dressage, Tetrathlon and Mounted Games (the Prince Philip Cup). These Area competitions serve as the qualifying rounds for the National Championships in each of these disciplines. The Championships for Horse Trials, Dressage and Showjumping are held at Weston Park in Shropshire at the end of August and those for Tetrathlon a week earlier, currently at Moreton Morrell in Warwickshire. For the Mounted Games, there is an additional tier known as the Zone Finals, which qualifies for the Finals held at the Horse of the Year Show at Wembley in October. Polo and Polocrosse also have Championships, but these are organised on a different basis because of the smaller number of branches involved.

Part of the membership fee is retained by the branch for laying on rallies and other functions and part is sent to Pony Club Headquarters at Stoneleigh. From here, rules for each of the disciplines are drawn up and sent out, arrangements for competitions made, standards set for Pony Club tests, training courses and conferences for instructors and officials organised and much else besides. In addition, the membership fee includes a most valuable insurance package which gives the Club itself and the branch public liability cover and every member personal liability cover for 'accidental injury or damage to third parties or their property arising out of the use of ponies' or horses and vehicles drawn by them.

The Pony Club started in 1929, when every hunt in Britain was written to asking them to form a branch. Six months later the 14 founder branches were all in operation, and from then on it snowballed. There was some opposition when tests were first introduced, but standards initially were not as high as they are today: an 11-year-old succeeded in passing the A Test! The growth and development over the next 65 years was remarkable. The key figure in the early days was Colonel the Honourable Guy Cubitt, who started as District Commissioner of the Crawley and Horsham branch, was Chairman for a quarter of a

century and later became Life President. He considered one of his best qualifications for his role was the fact that his parents did not ride.

At branch level, the part played by the District Commissioner (the DC) is vital.
The DC of the Whaddon Chase, Mrs Jenny Dixey, was told 'Once you've been a
DC you can run a business, you could go into the diplomatic service, there is
actually virtually no job you cannot do.' She also says 'It's a full time job and
anyone who kids you otherwise is wrong.'

Mrs Patterson has been DC of the Hurworth Hunt branch in North Yorkshire
since 1979. 'Laughs are the best bit,' she says. 'If you haven't got a sense of
humour, don't do it. You should know a bit about horses, but, more important,
you have to like children.' She was herself a founder member of the branch, and
has seen many changes, 'and yet, basically, it is all the same, isn't it? I see a child
and I see probably its grandfather riding round. The seat doesn't seem to alter
much in a family. The odds are they've got slightly better ponies, even the tiny
ones. They are not as nasty: we used to get some very nasty ponies. The new,
non-riding families, sometimes they are very good and sometimes they are quite
maddening.' Often, she finds that where parents are 'a little bit stroppy', there
are other problems in the family, and once she is aware of this and able to show
understanding, on the Pony Club front 'it's all marvellous again'.

The main reason why local children who ride do not join is lack of transport, so
important in modern road conditions. 'A few years ago children would ride out
here if we were having a rally. Now if I hear one is going to ride I have 50,000
kittens. If one does happen to turn up who's hacked, I jolly well see it goes back in
somebody's box.'

Like most District Commissioners, she finds the constant ringing of the
telephone a major irritant, particularly for the rest of the family. At least, unlike
one DC, she has never had a call after midnight from a distraught mother asking
for detailed instructions on putting a bridle back together again, after taking it
apart to clean and failing to reassemble it before an event the following morning.
On the other hand, members who fail to communicate when they should can be
even more difficult: 'Children who arrive at rallies without prior notice risk not
receiving any instruction.'

Camp always brings its share of excitements: 'Some child fell off and kept the
bridle and the pony went off with the saddle across miles and miles of open moor'.

Appreciation sometimes comes from unexpected quarters. 'Somebody comes
up whom you haven't seen for years and years. You haven't a clue who they are,
but they say 'Do you remember we used to camp at so-and-so and do this and do
that and wasn't it lovely?' She may be leading a conventional life now but the one
thing she really remembers is the fun they used to have when they were in the
Pony Club. It's a very nice side of it. Probably they were very naughty at the time
and you thought they weren't enjoying anything and yet they were.'

Mrs Patricia Macneal has also been associated with the Pony Club all her life, as member, parent and now DC of the Blackmore and Sparkford Vale. Like many others, she feels that much has changed, with more going on for members, both in the Pony Club and elsewhere, and more and more smart competition ponies appearing. Yet the friendly spirit and enthusiasm persists, the foundation of a happy, successful branch. When a Mounted Games team from the United Pack branch recently stayed for a Zone Final, she found the old spirit of sportsmanship unaltered; members spend hours riding together, and really enjoying their ponies. There was jubilation when they qualified, as juniors, for Weston Park. She recently enjoyed the wedding of two former members who first met at Pony Club camp.

Mrs Christine Davies, who helps with the running of this large branch, also feels that the ponies are no longer all 'woolly jobs' and the park at events is now full of large lorries. 'For some it gets too serious. Parents put a lot of pressure on their children, especially if they've paid a lot of money for the four footed friend. It must be fun for everyone.' She still remembers how her now grown up daughter spent her ninth birthday. Her 11.2 pony Dinky became stuck on a stile type fence. 'Three men lifted him up bodily and put him down on the landing side, at which point the jockey remounted and went on to complete the course undeterred.'

Instructors too can find parental pressure difficult. Mrs Eeley in the Bicester remembers how as a B Test examiner 'I was almost intimidated by a parent whose daughter needed the B Test to go on to higher education at a horse college.' It can also be hard to explain to parents that they would be well advised to replace a saddle, or even the pony. The parent or child who seeks advice on bitting and asks 'What should I put it in?' does not want to be told 'Put it in a tin!'

Parents sometimes forget that Pony Club officials work long hours unpaid (or, in the case of some instructors, paid little more than expenses) to help their children. Many DCs appear acerbic, not all are models of tact and diplomacy. Members in one branch declare 'Until you're about 13 or 14 you think she's really horrible and then suddenly you develop the same sort of sense of humour and you discover that she's actually joking when she says things. Then you think that's quite funny.' Sometimes members are more appreciative than their parents of the people who make the Pony Club work.

— 2 —

THE NEW MEMBER

The Rice family do not usually have a Sunday newspaper, but that Sunday was so wet and miserable that Mrs Rice bought the *Express*. Glancing at it, she saw that there was a competition to win a pony. She pushed the paper under a table, hoping that 11-year-old Sarah would not see it.

Some weeks later, long after Sarah had gone to bed, the telephone rang. Her mother answered it. 'Don't get excited, but your daughter is one of the finalists for a competition,' said the voice. Once she was persuaded that this was not a joke, a short discussion took place.

Next day at lunch time there was a second call, this time for Sarah. Tears streamed down her face as she murmured 'Yes, yes. Thank you, thank you.' She had won a pony, the pony's keep for two years, all vet's and blacksmith's bills for the same period, weekly riding lessons, also for two years, tack, rugs, riding clothes and membership of the Pony Club.

This is not a too-good-to-be-true, happy-ending story. It really happened. Sarah, whose entry was one out of 28,000, is now a keen member of the Spooners and West Dartmoor Pony Club and the proud owner of Stanwell Follyfoot, known as Folly, the 14 hand pony chosen for her by Mrs Di James, the District Commissioner. Sarah's father (who had blithely counter-signed her entry saying, in just fifty words, why she wanted a pony: she concluded 'I dream of riding my own pony across the moor'), wondered aloud whether there was a cash option but conceded that 'if you put it into Sarah's perspective it was probably better than winning the pools; there is nothing she'd have wanted more. I suppose I grossly underestimated the impact it was going to have.'

For the lives of the whole family have changed. The newspaper acted conscientiously: the initial call late in the evening was in part to ensure that the pony was going to a suitable home where it would be welcomed and that the family was likely to keep it after the two years were up. More importantly, the paper established a system of back-up support and regular knowledgeable contact by involving the Pony Club. But perhaps no-one could fully have prepared the family for the difference it was going to make to them all. 'It does cause arguments, there's no two ways about it, because we are not all committed to horses. If there is an event, it is a whole week-end gone,' says her father.

Sarah's younger brother is now a member of the Pony Club himself, has made a lot of friends through it and rides a Shetland pony at the farm where Folly is

(l to r) Sarah Rice and Folly, Laura Evans, Heather Fell (whose mother Doreen Fell has Folly at livery) and Rachel Bragg, the Girls' Minimus team for the Spooners and West Dartmoor Tetrathlon, 1992, Sarah's first tetrathlon. The team was placed third. *(Photo courtesy of the* Tavistock Times Gazette*)*

kept. Sometimes he enjoys joining in but really prefers playing rugby. Whilst a move of house shortly before the win had ended Mr Rice's opportunities for spending his leisure time on a boat, 'I would not have bought this house with all the maintenance and the garden if we'd known that every weekend we'd be rushing to and from the farm getting up early to go to events and things.' Despite the scope of the prize, there have also been expenses: they now own a trailer and the Metro has been exchanged for a Range Rover. Holidays too have been sacrificed: the last one, a long-awaited visit to Disneyland, unfortunately co-incided with the arrival of Folly, so that Sarah was repeatedly asking 'How long do we have to be away?' Mrs Rice is now the Pony Club joint rally organiser, and fast becoming an expert on jumps – loading them, unloading them, painting them, judging them for events and watching her daughter negotiate them.

Despite this, no item of the £10,000 budget provided has been better spent than the small investment in Pony Club membership. The original selection of the pony was made by the District Commissioner – not a service normally provided by the Pony Club, but in itself more difficult even than a conventional purchase since Sarah was a complete beginner who had only been riding some three or four months. A pony was needed which Sarah would be able to ride straight away but would also be suitable as she became more competent. Since then, 'The thing that Sarah's benefitted from this year is a wealth of experience. It's lovely to know you can pick up a phone the minute you have a problem; they'll always sort you out and help in any way they can. Also she's been able to try so many things.' Sarah enlarges on this: 'If I hadn't been with the Pony Club I wouldn't even have learnt to jump and I'm doing so much cross-country and things.' She has taken part in tetrathlon, cross-country, hunter trials and dressage, passed her D and C Tests, been to both Junior and Senior Pony Club Camps and won her first cup with Folly.

Folly now lives on a farm in the middle of Dartmoor ten minutes from their home. The farm owner, a knowledgeable horsewoman, has become a close friend. Her daughter is a little younger than Sarah, but with her greater riding experience they are a well matched pair. The families met when Junior Pony Club Camp (where, her mother teases, Sarah 'should have had a rosette for the one that fell off most') was held at the farm. Before she had Folly, Sarah 'was in the school every week-end and I never ever went on a ride. It's just like a whole new world now.'

Competitions can sometimes be worrying. Mr Rice may find that his wife and daughter have 'shot off to the entry tent and I'm left with this thing that I don't like spinning round looking like its going to stove in the side of a BMW.' Sarah sometimes finds that her lack of experience compared with her contemporaries means that there are insufficient novice classes for her age. Her mother looks at the fences and wonders 'Can they do it?' But in the Pony Club 'There is always someone to say "Yes you can do it, Sarah, Folly will take you round".' Her mother recalls her first event: 'When she came over the last fence she gave me a great big smile and said "Oh, that was wonderful" and burst into tears.' Her father agrees: 'It's actually worked out very well.'

Jenny Allan of the Bicester and Warden Hill branch in Oxfordshire is 12. Like Sarah, her parents previously had little interest in horses, though her mother has always enjoyed them and was even briefly a Pony Club member in her own childhood, an experience she did not appreciate since her parents simply dropped her off and later collected her from a riding school gate. 'I remember taking my D Test: it absolutely terrified me. I'd never sat on this pony before and had to take a Test on it!' This memory coupled with the cost meant that Mrs Allan had no wish to push Jenny into riding, but her father says she was 'horse orientated from the moment she could speak.' Even in her push chair she wanted only to be taken to feed the ponies, and could talk of nothing else. Mrs Allan helped exercise ponies at a local polo yard and the owner allowed Jenny to ride his children's pony. He suggested that she should join the Pony Club.

Although the only people they then knew in the Pony Club were a family whose children had been in the same toddler group, somebody suggested that Mrs Eeley might be able to help them, as she was not only knowledgeable, an instructress, and farmed nearby, but she also had a daughter of similar age. Mrs Eeley when approached duly promised to take Jenny and her pony to the next rally. Her mother 'just shooed Jenny aged six or seven with this pony on to Sue Eeley's lorry when it arrived and waved her goodbye. I don't know what they must have thought of me, mother sending her daughter off on her first rally without even staying with her. I didn't know that parents went. And I didn't know Sue. My son was then three and I didn't know if he'd have been welcome.' As she now realises, they would all have been most welcome. Since then the family has never looked back. Both parents are now fully involved, as will be seen in the chapter on parents, with Mrs Allan the Junior Rally Secretary. Jenny has found other members most generous in lending her ponies when she has had soundness problems. She has passed her C Test and no longer goes to Junior Camp, but found her first Senior Camp 'really good fun'. She also enjoyed the long distance ride, a speciality of the Bicester branch, when they rode 82 miles in three days, sleeping in barns on the way with 'one straw bale between two of you.' She has made most of her friends through the Pony Club: 'I knew two people to start with and by the end of the day it was "OK, you can come over to my house during the holidays".' Mrs Allan feels that too many children can be seen at horse shows being pushed into riding against their will, but 'as long as Jenny goes on enjoying it as much as she does then I'll endeavour to afford it, but I wouldn't push her into it.'

For both Jenny and Sarah the decision to join the Pony Club was taken out of their hands. But older children who enjoy riding are sometimes uncertain as to whether they would like to join. Some of the older members in the Poole branch have every sympathy with this anxiety, but know from experience that it is misplaced. Karen White (18), Catherine White (17), Sarah Austin and Georgina Spicer (both 16) and Sarah King (15) were all in double figures before they joined and some of them were already into their teens. They explained the reluctance: 'A lot of people don't actually want to join because it's a shame but its got a sort of stereotype – lots of posh people there with lots of expensive horses, and if you've got a little pony that cost you a few hundred pounds you think "Oh no, I'll show myself up". But it's not like that at all when you actually join. You go to your rallies, you make friends: everyone's very much like you are. Everyone's really friendly towards you. At my first rally everybody started talking to each other because you just share an interest, something to talk about.'

For children from families with a Pony Club background, if they are interested in riding there is seldom any question about joining the Pony Club. For families who are new to ponies it is even more useful. For, as Mrs Allan remarked, 'If ever there's a problem there's a handful of people on the other end of the telephone. Phone them up and get advice. It gives you peace of mind knowing there are some experts there.'

— 3 —

PONY CLUB CAMP

For many members, Pony Club Camp is the highlight of the year. Thomas Berry is just fourteen and he and his friends Oliver Dale and Philip Baker would not miss the Fitzwilliam camp for anything: 'Camp's brilliant, it really is.' It is held on the race course at Brampton, where, in Thomas's opinion, the facilities are excellent. Not only is the Tote available for use as 'the lads' dorm' – there are usually about seven or eight boys out of a total of around fifty campers – but, whenever there is a spare moment, 'It's usually sprinkler fights 'cos all round the race course they've got sprinklers and stuff. We just hold them in one place and the girls are running towards you and they don't get any further.' However, honours are equally divided, for Thomas acknowledges that the girls always get their own back, with 'buckets and stuff.' Half an hour later, the opposing sides will be united against the unfortunate instructors. 'A couple of instructors join in, others stay down there and do their own thing. We got a few wet last year and I don't think they were too happy. We were against all of the instructors actually down at the stable yard. All the instructors were in their little cabin there and we were outside. We had buckets on the roof: soon as they walked out the door we got them. Quite funny really. Well, they got us back, so ... so long as they found the funny side.'

At the Fitzwilliam camp, children are divided into groups of around eight of comparable standard (at some camps there is a special 'boys' ride': Thomas,

Thomas Berry with Lady and Dusky, 1992 Winners respectively of Peterborough and District Riding Club 12.2 hh and 13.2 hh classes. *(Gillian Berry)*

The Craven Branch of the Pony Club Camp 1993.
(Pleasure Prints, Crookham Common)

Oliver and Philip are always in the same group) with an instructor allocated to each group or 'ride' for the week. They ride twice a day, with instruction; the morning ride is often mostly flatwork, with jumping usually in the afternoon. They will also be taught throughout camp the right way to look after their ponies, with a routine of feeding, mucking out, grooming and tack cleaning established for the whole camp, and each ride's instructor or instructress taking responsiblity for his or her group of children and ponies. In addition, each ride will be taught a range of skills appropriate to their age and standard so that they learn more about horses and ponies and work towards the next test in the Pony Club ladder. There will also be talks and lectures from outside speakers. Perhaps the local blacksmith, vet, feed merchant or saddler may come in to pass on some of his knowledge and experience, or an eminent local rider may give a talk. Sometimes, particularly at smaller camps because of the transport difficulties, there are visits to places of interest, such as a stud farm, the local hunt kennels or a professionally run yard, and in hot weather, a nearby swimming pool is always popular.

Thomas enjoys every aspect of camp. 'If the other boys dropped out I'd keep going. It's still as much fun really 'cos there's plenty of others – you get to know them quickly. I've made a lot of good friends through it'; indeed he first met Philip through the Pony Club. But Thomas not only enjoys the fun of camp, he also takes his riding seriously. He rides well and enjoys hunter trials, horse trials, showjumping and especially hunting. Particularly with his 12.2 pony Lady, whom he has now outgrown, he took a regular part in team showjumping competitions, representing the branch. Looking after the ponies at home is hard work: until recently he had two at home, his own old one and one on loan, and rode one in the mornings and one in the evenings. He always does everything himself: 'You get used to it, you get in a routine and you can't get out of it.'

Thomas regards the Pony Club as more than a hobby: he sees it as training for his future career. 'Oliver might take his father's business over, which is horse-shoes, and Philip – I think he wants to be a farmer 'cos his dad is one', but Thomas himself has set his heart on riding professionally, preferably as a steeplechase jockey. He is prepared to put considerable time and effort into anything connected with horses, whereas 'I never have liked school. I really do hate it. It's the worst thing ever made I'm sure. People say it's the best years of your life, but ...' He was delighted to be given the opportunity to gain work experience in an eventing yard: 'It's good fun there and you learn a lot', and it was particularly satisfying when the two horses from the yard each won its class at the Three-Day Event to which he accompanied them. But 'It's a kind of a toss-up between racing and eventing'; when he recently had the chance to ride out for a trainer, 'It was brilliant. I just like riding fast really. Steeplechasing is more fun, more exciting than flat racing.' He is hoping to spend a week shortly in the yard of one of the leading National Hunt trainers. Whilst he is not slow to take advantage of such opportunities ('Snapped it up quick!'), he has no doubts about where he has learnt most of what he knows: 'Camp and rallies and stuff.' Even tests he considers worthwhile: 'Well, you learn something, don't you?'

Piers and Marcus Vallance too, in the Bicester country, who are 14 and 15, look forward to camp each year. When Marcus was unable to ride because of a serious head injury caused by a fall, he still went to camp on a bicycle. 'I enjoy camp,' he says, 'everyone's so friendly and it's good fun, not so strict but there are rules to break!' Rules include a ban on alcohol, but the year when the instructors made the mistake of leaving the wine for their own final evening party outside their caravan will long be remembered in the Bicester. The week traditionally ends with a play put on by the members in which all the instructors are taken off: one particularly memorable performance starred Marcus as Red Riding Hood in 'Red Riding Hood goes to the Pony Club Ball'.

The balance between respect for instructors and having fun is not an easy one.

Some of the Poole members summed this up: 'It's difficult to think of the instructor as a human being as opposed to a teacher at school! But they're not frightening people: they take things as a joke. You know how far you can go with each instructor.' Their camp, sleeping in a loft, is shared, they convince each other, by rats, bats and birds. There are other natural hazards: the trap door had a mattress below it so that it could be used as a fire escape. Members could not resist leaving it open with a cushion concealing the hole for the next unwary camper.

The learning side is not neglected. 'You join the Pony Club and suddenly realise how much you don't know. Camp is a sort of crash course because if you don't do it the team members lay into you because you get so many black points.' It is always an exhausting week: 'Even though you're really tired you manage to stay up until about 12 o'clock talking and mucking around. I just automatically got up at seven the next morning to feed and muck out. I fell asleep every single night with my clothes on. The smell's really bad at camp. We used to wash at the yard tap. It's a real disappointment to go home. The horses are immaculate when they come home ...'

Some branches have a special separate Associates camp, or expect Associates to go to an Area Associates' Camp if there is one. The Poole camp does not seem to lose its appeal at this age. Karen White at 18 was going to be away and miss camp, but 'I wish I was going now. I keep thinking maybe I should.'

Most branches now have a Junior Camp as well as a Senior one. With the Poole, Senior Camp starts at around 11. Catie Batten, Sarah Morton, Tamasine Angell and Guy Tetley are aged between 10 and 13, so several of them have tried both camps, but 'Senior Camp is a lot more fun'. Although Junior Camp is by day only, the traditions of Senior Camp seem to have spread to it: the unfortunate Guy, whose birthday is during camp week, seems to celebrate it regularly with a ducking in the water trough: 'It's a slimey one too, and freezing cold!'. This group preferred non-competitive activities to competitive ones: they enjoy treasure hunts, rallies and hacks. Guy, who is not keen on jumping, particularly enjoys rides through the forest, and, even for the jumping enthusiasts, when they 'hired out a cross-country course and we went round with an instructor, that was much more fun than as a competition,' although Tamasine 'likes doing hunter trials and things.' On one memorable occasion they had a Cowboys and Indians Fun Day, dressed up, over a cross-country course.

Sarah Harrington, Ross Angell and Leo Tetley are nine and Victoria Coles just seven. Unlike those who have tried both camps, they enjoy their Junior Camp and are not looking forward to moving up: 'They sleep in a barn. I prefer to sleep in a house. There might be thunder, and it's not warm.' They look forward more to branch outings: 'Olympia was fun. I missed school to go – I had to say I was ill.' They had also walked the course at Badminton: 'I could jump those fences!'

The West Hampshire branch does not have separate Senior and Junior camps.

Even mucking out
can be fun.
(Iain Burns)

Water fights, duckings in a filthy trough and the burying of teddies in the muck heap are all popular pastimes. To be the victim of such pranks and practical jokes must be a doubtful pleasure. Yet no-one is reluctant to go as a result. The secret of a successful camp is an atmosphere where the jokes are always made in a friendly spirit, and everyone has a turn at ducking as well as being ducked. Even the West Hampshire member who, the first time she came to camp, found her pony dressed up as a punk and sprayed blue and green with chains round his neck thought it great fun. Another recalls with amusement how 'Three years in a row they bought me a dummy because I sucked my thumb.'

'Our branch has got a good reputation for being friendly,' says Kate Dymond who is 15. 'Everyone knows each other. I expected it to be really snobby and everyone on these expensive ponies and stuff and its nothing like that at all.' Other happy memories include the boys who mistakenly used neatsfoot hoof oil on their saddles, the washing up routine ('I got an award for the best dryer up and I got a little badge'), games dipping faces into water first and then bran, and toothpaste fights: 12-year-old Ben Broomfield returned home with his wash bag unopened but his tube of toothpaste quite finished. One particularly riotous evening was concluded with campers setting out at 1 a.m. to find helpers stationed all over the common making different animal noises in the dark. It was a race to find them all, with helpers signing each camper's sheet of paper when found.

The proximity of the New Forest makes this a particularly attractive part of the country in which to ride. This is especially appreciated outside camp week with rallies such as the 'Spider Ride', when members ride from their respective stables to an agreed point where they meet for lunch. There are also rallies on the beach with a barbecue.

Many of the parents take a keen interest. Yet Nick and Felicity Campbell (who are 17 and 12 respectively) come from a family with no previous interest in horses. Since Nick showed how keen he was, his mother has given him full support. His success in the tetrathlon is now being superseded by his enthusiasm for horse trials, and he has been taken on as a working pupil by Mark Todd. Felicity prefers horse trials to tetrathlon, as does 11-year-old Lucy Clarke. Catriona Broomfield, who is 11 and whose mother is a former member and is Chief Instructress, and 12-year-old Caroline Shipway both rate Camp as the best thing of all in the Pony Club. Fourteen-year-old Sophie Roe's mother is Pony Club secretary. Sophie is a real enthusiast: not only is she already in the horse trials team, but she is fully appreciative of the fun of Camp, as is evident from her photographs showing her 11-year-old sister Polly washing her hair under the tap and two other campers in the trough.

Camp provides an opportunity for Associates to become involved as helpers or instructresses. In the West Hampshire, Jo Lister continues to go to Camp, but now she is a 'nanny'. In the Four Burrow branch in Cornwall, Fiona Tolhurst, another 18-year-old, was also helping the DC with camp. Fiona has already pased her H Test and is working towards her A. She has also passed her BHSAI exam and has started to give some private lessons: 'I like teaching the little ones best.' Fiona used to belong to the Prince Philip Cup team, and has been to the Championships for Dressage, Horse Trials and Showjumping. In 1993 the Horse Trials team was 7th and the Showjumping team 11th. Although she really prefers Horse Trials, she is currently doing more showjumping because, outside the Pony Club, it is less expensive. She has schooled a number of young horses herself, and in winter she works with the hunt horses, as well as hunting the young horses: 'I find it always helps them; lose hunting and you'd lose a lot of good horses as well.'

Emma Perkins too enjoyed the Pony Club: 'I had a great time, I loved it,' and retains many of her Pony Club friends. Perhaps she is glad that she is now too old, though, for having her mother as an instructress was bad enough: 'There

(right) Polly Roe washing her hair at the West Hampshire Camp. (Sophie Roe)

(below left) A member of the Craven branch with her pony. (Pleasure Prints, Crookham Common)

(below right) Fiona Tolhurst and her horse Onas Mona. (Iain Burns)

Four members of the Woodland Branch at Camp 1993.
(Pleasure Prints, Crookham Common)

Cotswold Pony Club Camp. *(Bob Langrish)*

was one tearful point in camp when mum was first teaching there, a bit melodramatic: "How could a daughter of mine do that when I am teaching here?"' What she did she does not say. Her mother is now DC, and perhaps thankful that there is a different group at Four Burrow camps. 'The night before the final day's event we used to go round with brushes and paint, painting slogans on the jumps. Then another lot would go round and cross out bits. We took a car and put it in the middle of the cross-country course, in the middle of a double, then someone completely lost the keys. Camps were absolutely great: they used to be quite tough. I used to go with a broken collar bone which was the best thing because you didn't have to do any of the riding, just sit in the car watching the lesson! I got in the dressage team once and came last out of the whole Area! Bucking and rearing the whole way through. That was my team career! Boots either did a brilliant dressage test or an absolutely awful one. He had to lose his temper beforehand and unfortunately we got there a bit late!'

Emma was in fact also in many other teams, including the tetrathlon team which eventually came fifth at the Championships. Even when she was small, she was more conscientious than she implies, although efforts occasionally misfired. At her first camp, 'I knew I was not going to get round the cross-country course on the last day so me and my really good friend got up at four o'clock and got our ponies out and thought we'd go and do the cross-country course, because we knew that there was absolutely no way we'd get past the first fence. So we were in the far field when everyone else was getting up, and they could see these two greys galloping up . . .'

'Yes, greys are hopeless!' someone commented.

'This one was!' replied Emma. 'Later on I didn't get past the first fence!'

— 4 —

WHAT TO WEAR

The most important item of dress is the hat. For all Pony Club activities it is essential that this meets the BSI standard 4472. However high the standard, no hat can reach it, or indeed be effective at all, unless the chinstrap is always properly fastened whenever you are sitting on a pony or horse, however briefly. If there is a drawstring inside, this also must be properly tied. If a hat has been involved in a bad fall, it is usually wise to replace it. You may choose either a hat which meets the correct standard but is velvet on the outside in the style of the old hunting caps, or a jockey's skull which will need to be worn with a 'silk'. Silks should be worn with the peak horizontal, covering the whole hat, and velvet caps must never be worn on the back of the head. In either case the velvet or silk must be either black or navy blue, except for cross-country and mounted games. If you have the velvet style, you will still be able to wear a coloured silk on top for these occasions. Your hair underneath the hat must be neat and tidy, and, for girls (or long haired boys), should be worn in a hairnet. Never allow any hair to protrude at the front of the hat, and it should be neatly fixed in the net across your ears. Any resemblance to a Yorkshire Terrier should be avoided. If you have very long hair, it looks much smarter if you wear it in a neat bun. Never wear earrings: not only do they look incorrect, but they are dangerous as they can easily get caught and tear your ears.

Next most important from a safety point of view are the boots. Whenever you are riding, avoid wearing Wellington boots or other shoes or boots with ridged soles designed for walking: if you have a fall they can easily be caught in the stirrup so that you are dragged. It is equally important to have a raised heel: trainers are very dangerous as your foot can slide right through the stirrup. Jodhpur boots are ideal, but if you do not have any, walking shoes with smooth soles and raised heels are acceptable. Older members will probably want to wear long riding boots: whilst leather is the ultimate ideal, they are extremely expensive and certainly not a wise buy until you have finished growing. Rubber ones are suitable. If you do have leather boots, you should have garter straps, buckled at the front of your knee, with the spare end of the strap to the outside. Whatever sort of boots you have, make sure they are clean and shiny.

Spurs should only be worn when the Chief Instructor advises that you have a truly independent seat. They must have blunt ends, which point downwards.

Katie Britten of the Fernie Hunt Branch correctly dressed
for Pony Club activities. *(James Buxton)*

Rubber boots are often shaped at the back of the heel to show where the spur should fit. The outside of the spur is longer than the inside, the strap buckle is on the outside and if there is a long spare end on the strap, it should either be cut off or tucked in.

Jodhpurs or breeches should be fawn coloured for smart use, including rallies if possible, although navy blue is practical at home. For competitions, except for the Prince Philip Cup and cross-country (but including hunter trials where correct hunting dress is often specified), a tweed jacket is usually preferable to a navy blue or black jacket. Avoid any form of coloured trimmings or velvet collars, and in particular avoid coloured tack for your pony. For rallies and dressage, a plain white or blue shirt and a Pony Club tie (pale blue, gold and purple), pinned down to prevent it flapping in the breeze, is excellent. If you are jumping fences, a hunting tie (this is its correct name though it is often referred to as a stock) gives some protection to your neck if you have a fall. Such a tie can also be used in an emergency as a bandage for person or horse, or as a sling. It should be white if you are wearing a navy blue or black coat and coloured, usually checked or spotted, with a tweed jacket. Tie it in a double knot neatly but tightly or it cannot do its job, and fasten it with as many pins as you need underneath and one straight bar pin on top.

Many branches are happy for you to wear a plain, dark sweat shirt for rallies. This is more comfortable and helps your instructor to see if you are sitting correctly. You may be able to buy a sweat shirt with your branch name and the Pony Club logo on it. However hot the weather, do not have short sleeves: a fall on bare arms can be uncomfortable. Gloves are often helpful, and light coloured ones are compulsory for some dressage tests. Always check the relevant rule book for any special rules about dress or tack.

If you are jumping fences, for competitions it is essential and for rallies and schooling advisable to wear a body protector. New ones are numbered to show how much protection they give. Choose an effective one, but not one so bulky that you cannot move properly.

For the cross-country phase in horse trials or tetrathlon, you can be more imaginative in your choice of colours for jerseys and silks. Plain bright colours or spots, quarters or stripes are acceptable here. If you are in a team, your branch may have special branch colours.

For the Prince Philip Cup, you will have team colours. Ask your team trainer about this, and also about suitable dress for polo and polocrosse.

Finally, wear your Pony Club badge, polished to look really shiny, on your jacket. If you have passed the BHS Road Safety Test you may wear that badge too: the Pony Club Road Safety Test does not have a badge. You should also wear a felt or plastic disc in the appropriate colour to show which Pony Club test you have passed underneath your Pony Club badge.

This may all sound complicated: with experience, it is simpler than it sounds. Make sure everything is as neat, clean and plain as possible, and above all give yourself as much protection as possible when choosing and remembering to wear your hat, back protector, boots and hunting tie.

Pony Club Camp: *(above)*
Mucking out *(Iain Burns)*
and *(left)*, Victoria Meacher
and Janine Paterson in the
water trough at the West
Hampshire Camp *(Sophie
Roe)*

PLATE ONE

(left) Mounted Games (Pleasure Prints, Crookham Common)

PLATE TWO

(below) Joanne Syckelmoore on Pepi at the Mounted Games (see page 35) (David Stephens)

THE MOUNTED GAMES FOR THE PRINCE PHILIP CUP

The lights are dimmed, a horn blown, then as the Arena party race to set up lines of poles, buckets and balls in a fresh blaze of light, the watching children burst into a roar, cheering, screaming and chanting the name of the team they have come to support. This is the Horse of the Year Show at Wembley, where the six Pony Club teams from all over the United Kingdom who have won through Area and Zone heats to the Mounted Games Championship are battling it out for the Prince Philip Cup.

One team has won the Cup eight times since 1978: the Eglinton team from Ayrshire in Scotland. In 1993 Marion Nairn was the captain. It was her third and last visit to Wembley, for in 1994 she will be too old: in 1991 the team was second, then they won it in both the succeeding years. This was particularly creditable in 1993, for Marion was the only team member to have been to Wembley before, and 'the rest of them get more nervous'.

Mr Robert Noble, the team trainer, agrees. 'Experience does away with nerves.' He started training the team in 1976. In 1977 they first went to Wembley, and won a year later. Since then they have reached the Championships every year except 1985. 'You win things by hard work, devoted parents, a wee bit of knowledge and a good bit of discipline,' he says.

Marion first started the Games when she was about seven. The branch usually has at least two Senior and two Junior teams. Training starts in January on a Sunday, then, Mr Noble explains, when the clock changes 'Everybody in our team knows that a Tuesday and a Thursday night throughout the summer are training nights, unless somebody's got the 'flu or there's something wrong with them. You canna go anywhere else on a Tuesday night. If one said "We canna come" and the next time another "We canna come" then you're not training as a team. They've got to understand there's a tremendous commitment.'

The special magic of Wembley exerts a strong fascination. 'The Games are the only thing in the Pony Club that takes you to the Horse of the Year Show. Wembley means something.' When one Eglinton member broke her leg a fortnight before Wembley one year everyone felt for her. Fortunately she was young enough to be able to go the following year. However the actual week is a further demand on parents in both time and money. Each family takes a horsebox or caravan and they travel down in convoy. Staying with friends is not acceptable, and the original system of team members sharing a single caravan did not prove

The Eglinton Prince Philip Cup team with Mr Noble at Perth 1991: Marion Nairn second rider from left. *(Martin Pawson)*

satisfactory. Different tastes in food and the need to have somewhere to go away on their own if they had a bad run made it better for each child to be with their own family.

During the week at Wembley, 'You're on every day, sometimes twice. That's the great thing about it: you can spend £20,000 on a showjumping pony and you kick a fence down and that's you.' However the week goes, four of the six teams compete at every performance on a pre-arranged rota, with only the final night reserved for the leading four teams, culminating for the winning team in the lap of honour with the spotlight shining on them.

Teams are made up of five members from the same branch, and each must have been under fifteen at the beginning of the year. Ponies have to be under 14 hands 2 inches, though heavier children are not allowed to ride very small ponies. Each race usually involves four members of each team so that ponies take turns at having a rest, though their riders may be needed on foot to hold other ponies. Every year rules are laid down for a selection of races with names such as the Five Flag Race or Postman's Chase, which usually involve the completion of certain tasks by each member of the team in succession as a form of relay race. The speed and accuracy with which objects are placed on posts or in containers, flags moved or batons handed over is quite bewildering to the newcomer, but thrilling to watch and a real challenge to the competitors.

Whilst competing at Wembley is the ultimate dream of every team member, and of thousands more children besides who have never sat on a pony, just thirty children a year have the chance. For hundreds of others, the build-up towards the Area competitions and perhaps the Zone Finals as well as a selection of 'friendly' and invitation matches, will provide excitement and fun.

Joanne Syckelmoore has never competed at Wembley, but her skill at Mounted Games has won her a starring role on the television programme 'You Bet'. Unlike many PPC competitors, she did not join the Pony Club to take part in the Games, but discovered the Games after spending some time benefitting from other aspects of the Pony Club. Her mother thinks that is important for both the child and the pony. 'A lot of ponies have got very hard mouths from a lot of yanking about. I think what it boils down to is if they've been taught the basics before they do a lot of PPC it's always there. They have been taught that ponies don't have to be pulled or roughed about to do what you want them to do.'

Brought up on a farm with horses and ponies, Joanne and her older sister Katherine both joined the Garth South branch at an early age. Gordon Cook has trained the branch Prince Philip Cup teams for many years with flair and enthusiasm, and persuaded the two girls to come to a practice session one Sunday. Joanne thoroughly enjoyed herself but her sister was less enthusiastic. After both had taken part for a year they decided not to continue the following

A Mounted Games Competitor. *(Iain Burns)*

A Prince Philip Cup
team cleaning tack
at the Horse of the
Year Show 1987.
(Bob Langrish)

year, but to concentrate on showjumping instead. However Joanne was later
asked to come back when a team member was put out of action by an injury three
weeks before the Area competition. Joanne was included in the 'B' team that
year and progressed from there.

However her own pony 'absolutely hated' the Games. Fortunately the team
trainer was later able to lend her an outgrown pony of his daughter's, which was
getting old but proved marvellous for learning on. Whilst the Prince Philip Cup
was designed, in the words of the rule book, for 'ordinary children on ordinary

ponies', Joanne has found from experience that the most successful Games ponies 'on the whole don't jump'. This makes it difficult for a girl like Joanne who enjoys showjumping, hunter trialling and hunting as well as mounted games. It was not until her last two years in the sport that she actually had a pony of her own suitable for the competitions, but the grey Pepi lived and breathed for the games. 'I mean, she's gone to rallies as required but only just to qualify her, you can't take her to learn anything. The ride I would normally go in is not suitable for Pepi. I did take her in a small Hunter Trials once. I'm never doing that again: it was just a total failure. The gate was immaculate – I've never done a gate so fast.'

For ponies like Pepi speed is everything: 'She only gives you a couple of seconds and if you haven't done it by then you're too late.' The most successful ponies are usually about 13.2. Smaller ponies are seldom sufficiently fast, but bigger ponies can be difficult to vault on to quickly enough. When Joanne first had Pepi she found that 'I used to get dragged along because I wasn't ready for her to go flat out.'

Team members have to be prepared to work hard. Training starts in January with general skills, fast turns, vaulting on and so on. Then the particular races appointed for that year have to be learnt and practised and the members have to learn to work together as a team. Joanne sees this as the most important aspect. 'There is very much team spirit in Pony Club teams,' she says. 'The ideal team rides for each other. Some teams are very friendly. When we went to Wales we spent our whole time with the South Berks. In our Area all the teams are friendly, even if you don't like them you're nice to them. Some Mounted Games teams (outside the Pony Club) are horrible to each other. You can't ride for your own glory can you? You've got to consider the person you're galloping into the way you hand over, haven't you? If they're leading their pony and got to vault on you've got to give them that chance, you can't just gallop on and say "Well, come on, why didn't you get on?"'

Yet the Prince Philip Cup is sometimes criticized for encouraging roughness and thoughtless riding. This is much less likely to happen with children who have learnt to ride properly before starting to compete. The right pony also makes a difference, for ponies with hard mouths make children with heavy hands as surely as children with bad hands ruin ponies' mouths. Pepi has a very soft mouth but when Joanne rode a friend's pony, the hot, tense pony was causing Joanne's hands to deteriorate, until she came back to Pepi. On the other hand, Mrs Patterson, DC of the Hurworth, thinks that the Games often improve children's riding, particularly with the sort of child 'who "sits so beautifully", and as soon as the pony moves sideways the child is still in the correct position, but on the ground.'

The sport certainly attracts a number of extroverts. Joanne and her mother still smile as they remember the antics of one team member at the Royal Welsh

Show. After dismounting to pick up a sock during the sock race, he lost his balance before he could vault back on, just as the pony was breaking into a canter. With commendable presence of mind, he grabbed it by the hock, then turned to the crowd to execute a perfect bow before vaulting on.

The television crew for the programme 'You Bet' were not looking for a born clown, but for a friendly, forthcoming, smiling and sensible competitor to match, not against another rider, but against a child handler with an agility dog. Whilst jumping is not Pepi's strongest suit, unlike some of the other ponies she was willing to jump round a two foot six course, and she and Joanne were selected to go to Burghley and be filmed. Joanne and her mother were put up in an hotel, whilst Pepi stayed in a loose box 'as big as this room' at Burghley House. After a day becoming accustomed to the delays involved in the world of television, the contest proved challenging. The course was designed rather for the dog, a most attractive, reddish coloured collie, than the pony, and at first Pepi could only trot through bending poles placed five yards apart instead of the customary ten, but soon she was flying through, changing legs at every stride.

In the practice they beat the dog, which was beside itself with excitement, but in the final performance Joanne just failed to fasten the gate correctly – a considerably easier task for the dog handler – and was beaten. The filming was not complete: a further session followed in a studio with an enthusiastic audience. Pepi showed her true star quality by crossing a strange coloured, hollow sounding floor, stepping over a channel for a sliding door onto a brilliantly lit stage in lurid colours to a loudly applauding audience, and taking everything in her stride.

A young Mounted Games competitor. *(Bob Langrish)*

— 6 —

PARENTS

It is a favourite joke amongst DCs that the Pony Club would be a marvellous institution if only the children were orphans: parents are seen as causing more trouble than children. On the other hand, without parents the Pony Club would soon cease to exist, for it is entirely dependent on voluntary help and parents are the people with a vested interest in supplying that help. However, some do not see things in this way: at one rally when parents were invited to put away the jumps at the end, a father replied, 'I've paid my subscription. I'll let someone else clear it up', and stumped away with his child. Whether he imagined that other parents had not paid their subscriptions is not clear.

Being a good Pony Club parent is both demanding and time-consuming. First comes the commitment, financial, practical and moral, to child and pony. In modern traffic conditions, it is rarely safe for the child to hack to Pony Club functions. A driver will be needed, or arrangements made for sharing lifts. Looking after the pony at home may be the child's responsibility, but even so some supervision is essential, and practical support will be needed in times of illness or exams. The Pony Club can help by providing a network of knowledge-able people to whom to turn.

Secondly, the Pony Club is a labour-intensive operation. Parents should be prepared to put in their fair share of effort. With the exception of some in-structors, nobody at branch level is paid. Laying on a full holiday programme of education and entertainment is a major undertaking. When it is left to a tiny minority of adults, not all of whom necessarily even have children of their own to benefit, the burden becomes too great. There are many different ways in which parents can help. The ideal situation is for parental skills to be matched to appropriate tasks, most easily achieved by parents volunteering. Those handy with a hammer and nails can offer assistance with course building, good cooks can produce meals for camp, mathematicians may be able to help with scoring at events, and so on.

When Mark Colvin joined the Stanmore branch, his father had almost forgot-ten that when he himself was an apprentice engineer he was required to take up a sport and chose fencing. Then Mark became interested in the tetrathlon and his father found that by coaching all interested members in fencing, he enabled them to take part in pentathlons as well as tetrathlons.

The tetrathlon is a field which allows many fathers and mothers to contribute in a special way. Mr Ferens is a veterinary surgeon whose two sons Tim and Michael belong to the Bicester branch. He organises the tetrathlon for the branch, and, having had a lot of experience at rifle shooting when he himself was at school, teaches pistol shooting. Despite his own skill, he had not previously attempted to teach others, but, with the aid of his niece who had won a blue as Ladies Captain of the Oxford University Modern Pentathlon team, soon acquired the necessary ability. For the August Bank Holiday each year he and his wife organise a camping weekend in the Beaufort country for around 20 members who are tetrathlon enthusiasts, taking caravans, tents and ponies.

Mrs Ferens too has taken on many other new duties, cooking, helping at camp and even becoming involved with course building mid-week when few fathers are able to come: one of the fences on the course has been named Anne's Lattice after her. She actually learnt to ride when Michael was a baby in case he became interested, and now helps with the exercising. She also had to cope when Michael had an horrendous fall, fortunately whilst wearing a skull cap, and was unconscious for six hours. The friend who drove them to hospital was impressed with her seeming calm: her own recollections of her feelings are somewhat different. Mr and Mrs Ferens certainly combine support, both practical and moral, for their own sons with a positive contribution to the branch in general.

There are a large number of jobs which almost anyone can do: moving show jumps, the perennial nightmare of DCs and Secretaries, becomes relatively simple when there are enough people available in the right place at the right time. Fence judging at an event, hunter trial or tetrathlon is another useful contribution. Helpers sit, usually in their cars, beside a particular cross-country fence, recording what takes place, a responsible job, for many of the arguments at the end of the day will centre on what actually happened and whether it was accurately marked. The fence judge too will be the nearest person in case of an accident, although an ambulance and First Aiders will be present.

Becoming involved is one of the best ways for a parent to make friends with other parents and officials. For sometimes the new parent can find the hierarchy somewhat intimidating. Mrs Myatt found this when Louisa and Emma first joined the Bicester. 'I remember the very first rally we turned up to, I'm sure she didn't mean to do it but I was told off because the kids were riding in anoraks. Quite right, but we didn't have any hacking jackets. It was two years before I actually called the Secretary or DC by their Christian names and that kept a barrier going really.' Now that Mrs Myatt is herself involved in the organisational side, she tries hard to get parents involved. 'In the end you need the parents. There are so many more non horsey families coming in. It's about helping those parents, encouraging them to come to an all-day rally and join in something like a lungeing demonstration, and have a glass of wine together.' Possibly Mrs Myatt found her introduction particularly difficult because she works full-time so was seldom able to come.

Mr Myatt, on the other hand, farms and, say his daughters, 'He comes to everything: he's brilliant in the Pony Club. Most of the fathers don't come except for the major competitions. He comes along and gets entertained by all the Pony Club mums. He's wonderful with horses, got the magic touch. He doesn't ride himself but he picks up lots of things that he tells us.' But at home in the evenings, 'Mum helps a lot. She always arranges lessons for me' and at exam times she is ready to step in and do the horses: 'We all muck in together.'

In the same branch, the Allan family found themselves entering a new world when, a few years later, Jenny joined. In the intervening years, the atmosphere had become more relaxed. Mrs Allan, a school secretary, is now Junior Rally Secretary, as well as spending much time helping Jenny to look after the pony at home. 'The Pony Club is very sociable. I've known nothing but kindness.'

Mr Allan helps to build cross-country courses. 'I'm a practical sort of person. They were asking people to help so I went along and enjoyed it. I don't know anything about horses, but I can put bits of wood together.' He works with the

'Parents should be prepared to put in their fair share of effort.'

course designer, and 'on the actual day of the event there's a good deal of satisfaction in it.'

Being a parent inevitably carries its share of anxieties. Jenny's mother recalls the occasion when Jenny was kicked on the foot during Junior Camp. She was limping that evening, but the suggestion of a hospital visit silenced her moans and they resorted instead to a packet of frozen peas on the injury. Next morning she took part in a mounted display for parents before hobbling up at Prize Giving to collect numerous trophies, including a cup for the most helpful and pleasant person in camp. It was only during a celebratory meal that evening that a hospital visit became essential and the foot was found to be broken, remaining in plaster for the rest of the summer.

The Pony Club is often seen as something which mothers and daughters enjoy, but which sons will only take part in under protest. That has certainly not been the case with the Berry family in the Fitzwilliam branch. Neither of Thomas's parents was very interested in horses. His mother had been brought up on a riding school, but her sister and brother had always been the keen, enthusiastic ones. When she bought a Shetland for Thomas perhaps she hoped that he would soon make clear his dislike of riding so that she could feel she had given him the chance then gracefully retire from the equestrian scene. But from the moment he first rode the Shetland, Thomas was constantly begging to go out on him. At first, Thomas remembers, she would reply '"Oh, not today" sort of thing, then she got used to it and she walked out with me and ... good fun!' Since then neither mother nor son has looked back. His mother has had almost as much enjoyment from his sport as Thomas has done, and has always given him the fullest backing.

Parents who make DCs dream of a branch consisting solely of orphans come in several types. Some are ignorant and unthinking, like the mother who, not having a trailer, tied the pony to the back of the car to drive it to gymkhanas. Others are conspicuous only by their absence, using the Pony Club as a creche for older children. Others, in the words of Malcolm Clapson of the Staff College and Sandhurst Hunt branch, 'are much more competitive than the children are. Some parents push the kids too hard which is a shame really because they don't get as much enjoyment out of it, they just push them into riding generally when they don't really want to at all.' This can lead in turn to aggressive behaviour at competitions and vocal arguments with officials. From there it is but a small step to becoming the sort of parent for whom the Pony Club has found it necessary to add a new rule: 'Unseemly behaviour on the part of parents will not be tolerated. Under certain circumstances adults who behave in an unseemly manner may be banned from attending Pony Club functions.'

Altogether being a Pony Club parent is a minefield. The only sensible conclusion was that reached in a poem originally published in *Horse and Hound*:

Pony Club Parents
(with apologies to Noel Coward)

Don't put your daughter on a pony, Mrs Worthington,
Don't put your daughter on a horse!
Or else you'll find your both her
Stable-lad and chauffeur,
With many other jobs to do of course.

You will stand for hours in slickers
With mud up to your knickers,
To watch her do her dressage in the rain.
You will get back home to dry out
And before you've time to cry out,
You'll be saddling up and starting out again.

You'll be up before its light
And be grooming half the night,
And never have a moment that is free.
You may snatch a quick banana
'Twixt events at a gymkhana,
But otherwise you'll live on flasks of tea.

While she is hunting foxes
You'll be mucking out the boxes,
Or towing trailers round the countryside.
If you find a moment idle
You can always clean a bridle,
While you wonder why you ever let her ride.

When the holidays are over
And the pony's out to clover,
And you think you'll have a decent night in bed,
You won't! – for what a pity
You've been put on the Committee
Planning torment for the holidays ahead.

Then you'll argue about fences
Till you nearly lose your senses,
And the proper way to build a jumping course.
When all resign then maybe
You'll be left to hold the baby!
No, don't put your daughter on a pony, Mrs Worthington,
Don't put your daughter on a horse!

B.P.H.

HORSE TRIALS

The Horse Trials Championship at Weston Park is the Pony Club's equivalent to Badminton or Burghley. It is a One-Day Event rather than a Three-Day Event, which means that the Roads and Tracks and Steeplechase phases are omitted, but the three important phases, Dressage, Cross-country and Showjumping, will all be completed by every competitor.

The Horse Trials Championship is the oldest and probably still the most sought after award in the Pony Club. The Team Championship was first introduced in 1949, with individual titles for both seniors and juniors awarded from 1963. Three years after this, the number of entries led to the junior individuals being divided into sections, so that there are now four junior individual winners of equal standing: in horse trials comparisons are never made between competitors whose dressage is judged by different judges, and there is a limit to the number of dressage tests which a particular judge can be asked to assess.

Sophie Allison of the Garth South was eight years old when she was interviewed for a television programme. She declared her admiration for Captain Mark Phillips and Lucinda Green, saying 'I like the three-day event and I might want to do it.' Her ambitions, she said, were 'to do eventing like at Badminton and hopefully, if I could, go to the Olympics.' Nine years later, she became British Junior Champion at the Windsor Three-Day event and only missed automatic inclusion in the Junior European Championships because her horse, Hillside Ghost, at six is a year too young. She has moved a long way towards fulfilling her unchanged ambitions. Sophie has always known what she is aiming for and pursued her goals with single-minded determination.

Sophie's first hunter trial was when she was five, on a pony originally bought for her brother. She remembers her father following her round the course on a motorbike, and picking her up after a fall at the log pile. She has always benefitted from strong family support. Her grandfather Douglas Gray was Director of the National Stud and rode in the Grand National, her grandmother was for many years DC of the Newmarket and Thurlow branch and her mother has been Rally Organiser for the Garth South for a long period.

Whilst horse trials were always her first love, at the remarkably young age of eight she represented her branch as an Individual in the Area Dressage competition. Her greatest successes at that time, though, were not in the Pony Club,

Sophie Allison starting her career with Ashlands Amanda. *(Bob Langrish)*

but with her Working Hunter Ponies, and in particular her 12.3 part bred Welsh pony Ashlands Amanda, rated the best part bred Welsh pony in the country in four consecutive years.

Meanwhile, Sophie and Amanda were regularly competing in the junior One-Day Events which have become a speciality of many branches of the Pony Club, affording the ideal introduction to horse trials for members from as young as seven or eight. No doubt her competitive experience in the show ring stood her in good stead as did her cross-country experience out hunting. 'I like hunting,' declares Sophie. 'You get all these fences; you don't really see them and you just keep going. I think it's wonderful and it really gets you to know your horse as well.' At present Sophie is unable to hunt because 'eventing you have to give them a holiday sometime.'

At 12, Sophie took part as an individual in her first Inter-Branch Area Horse Trials, the tiny Amanda incredibly coping with the enormous course, where fences can be up to 3 ft 6 in. in height and, for table type obstacles, in width. Fences with a ditch can have a spread of up to 7 ft. However, Amanda was deemed too small to be included in a Branch team, and next year Sophie graduated to a bigger pony.

Eventually Sophie had two outstanding ponies of between 14 hands and 14.2, both chestnuts. In 1990, when she was 15, she was third individual on Oxnead Little Luwe in her section in the Horse Trials Championships at Weston Park, and rode Westfalia Metatron in her branch Showjumping team which also came third at Weston Park. Metatron was equally successful as an eventer. The problems of combining horse trials with Working Hunter Pony classes were highlighted when one pony was listed for the International Pony Three-Day event team but was finally rejected as being 'a little too portly', inevitably since he was due to compete at the Royal Show the following week. The other pony came equally close to selection, but unfortunately contracted a virus at the vital moment.

The experience Sophie obtained from Pony Club events enabled her to compete in her first Junior BHS event at the age of 14, but even now at 18 she continues to take an active part in the Pony Club. She is training with Ruth McMullen, but, before moving to her yard, virtually all her instruction came either from Pony Club rallies, which she seldom missed, or from private lessons with the Chief Instructress for her branch, Sarah Ward. Sophie found the Pony Club tests worthwhile ('If you fail a test keep going like I did') and the opportunity to ride as part of a team invaluable for the future, she hopes! She sums it up: 'It's good, Pony Club. Stick with it and go to all your rallies. You learn a lot and meet a lot of people. It's good fun.'

Many members find that the best instructor they ever have has four legs, not two. The right pony or horse can teach his rider a remarkable amount, and, unlike even the most dedicated human teacher, he is always there when things are happening. Rosie Julian of the Four Burrow in Cornwall was just 14 when she first went to Weston Park to compete in both Horse Trials and Dressage. Many members reaching Weston Park for the first time find the cross-country course somewhat daunting, particularly those, like Rosie, from the more outlying areas of Britain. In many Pony Club Area competitions, particularly those in the Midland regions, the cross-country courses are comparable to Weston Park in size and scope, but there is a tendency in some parts where there are fewer competitors for the events to be somewhat lower key, making the transition to the Championships more of a shock. Inevitably it is often in the same areas that members have fewer events to compete in because of the distance.

However, Rosie, despite being one of the youngest competitors, knew her horse and 'thought it was OK when I walked it'. Charlie, her kind and experienced 15.2, had done it before with his previous owner, although Rosie had not encountered anything quite like the combination fences. The partnership proved superbly successful, jumping an excellent clear round. The day had given Rosie the experience as well as the confidence she needed for the future. Her

Into the water at the Horse Trials Championships at Weston Park 1991. *(Bob Langrish)*

interest in dressage, too, was stimulated by the horse's ability, inspiring her to practise schooling her old pony, who was then still in the family, in a manner she had not previously attempted.

For others, much of the appeal of horse trials is to bring on a young horse themselves, rider and horse learning together. Louisa Myatt (18), of the Bicester branch, and her sister Emma, who is two and a half years younger, did not join the Pony Club until Louisa was 11, when they first had transport for the ponies. Before that they hacked to the local Riding Club: 'I didn't really think of eventing before I joined the Pony Club, but it's just excellent for eventing. I joined to do a few more things. I'd got to the limit of the Riding Club, the Pony Club is much more competitive and we wanted to expand what we did with the ponies.' At first they found joining relatively late was somewhat difficult, and were glad to have each other. 'It does take a long time to build up friendships with people and get known. Camp is a good thing: you really get to know one another. That really was the turning point. We have teams right down to 11 and under and that was just fabulous. They'll put you in a team, it doesn't matter how good you are.'

Two years after she joined, her mother bought Louisa a five-year-old called Twizzle. 'When I first had her we couldn't canter a circle,' but Louisa persisted with her and Twizzle has now three times represented the branch at Area level

Louisa Myatt on Wellie at Weston Park. *(Pleasure Prints, Crookham Common)*

Horse Trials: *(above)* A competitor jumping the first fence at Area 6 Horse Trials *(A. & B. Sorohan: Event Prints)* and *(right)* Natalie Bucklar on By George (see page 50) *(Brian Bucklar)*

PLATE THREE

PLATE FOUR

(above) Hannah, Claire and Victoria Dingle with Megan (see page 52) *(Meriel Buxton)*, and (below) James Sorohan, who is profoundly deaf, aged 4 on Bobby *(A. & B. Sorohan: Event Prints)*

in dressage, once with Louisa and twice with Emma, and in 1993 she and Emma qualified for Weston Park as individuals. She has also been successful at Novice Pony Club events, but unfortunately lacks the scope to go on to Open ones. 'We had to learn everything together, with the help of the Pony Club. The Chief Instructor David Baker found her for us originally and has helped us all the way through. I fell off her I don't know how many times before I got the idea of the cross-country seat. She used to stop at the last minute and I came flying off, but she taught me an awful lot. That's the most fun if you've got a young horse and you bring them on yourself rather than having one that's done it all.'

Eventually, though, when Louisa outgrew Twizzle and he was passed on to Emma, she got a new young horse to start working on, but her mother also bought her Wellie, a retired BHS eventer with 25 points. Wellie, being old, was not expensive, and it is often possible for Pony Club members to find horses with experience in this way. 'She'd already had the challenge of bringing on a young horse. I was anxious to give her the chance to do the teams before she was too old and to get that bit more confidence.'

Louisa missed the Area Showjumping when Wellie was temporarily unsound, but the team qualified for Weston Park and when one member broke a collar-bone Louisa was able to go. She was also in the Horse Trials team for the qualifying Area round. Teams consist of four members with the best three counting. At the Area event, team spirit was strong. 'It's great being in the team, much more fun than just going round on your own. Everyone's rooting for each other. Everyone helps each other out. We were all feeding back information about the course.' Unfortunately one of them had a fall and had to withdraw during the cross-country phase, but Louisa did an excellent dressage and cross-country, and the other two team members were sufficiently well placed for the team to be certain of victory and a place in the Championships provided all three could go clear in the showjumping. Louisa was the first to jump. She seemed to be rattling every pole but her luck was in: her clear round won her a place in the Championships as an individual and provided an excellent start for the other two. The second team member went, and was also clear. Finally, it was the turn of the third and last Bicester member. She sailed round in superb style and left the ring to a storm of applause. Then a voice came over the loudspeaker: the last rider had mistaken a whistle elsewhere in the park for the starting bell. The bell had not been rung, she was therefore eliminated and the team was not even considered to have completed.

The attitude shown by everyone in the Bicester impressed Mrs Myatt deeply. Heartbreaking though it was, there was not one word of recrimination towards the unlucky girl, everyone was so sympathetic, and 'everybody was really rooting for this girl for the rest of the season.' This spirit is no doubt why Louisa feels 'It's great being in the team, it's really good fun. It's better winning as a team than as an individual; you can celebrate more.' Even as an individual, staying alone at Weston Park to compete in the Horse Trials on the two days after she had competed with the team in the Showjumping, she was delighted to find how many Bicester members bothered to drive 100 miles just to support her.

The joy of being part of a team is something which Natalie Bucklar misses with the Axe Vale, in Devon, for the branch does not have a team, just two individuals, competing at the Area Horse Trials. Mrs Sleight, the DC, and members alike emphasise that the Axe Vale is not at all competitive. On the other hand, the branch has an exceptionally friendly, helpful and supportive atmosphere. Natalie's talent is certainly developing in this relaxed, encouraging environment. As a small child she belonged to a different, highly competitive branch. As she did not then have an outstandingly successful pony and came from a non-horsey family, she felt that nobody was interested in her. But 'since I could walk I just wanted to learn to ride. When I first bought my pony when I was nine I kept her at the riding stables for about six months before we had the garage converted to a stable so we could have her at home.'

'I don't think she ever missed doing her pony on any filthy, foul winter's night or morning,' says her father.

'I want to go on now and get more serious. Mrs Sleight really does help me. She sends me all the schedules and gave up the whole day to give support for my B Test.' Natalie's last pony, Liberty, 'jumped anything in sight and I sort of progressed from there.' Soon she was proving most succesful in both horse trials and showjumping. Mrs Sleight then advised her when she was looking for a horse to move on to, and eventually helped her to find George, her current adored young horse, on whom she plans to continue Pony Club eventing and go on to BHS eventing as well.

Non-competitive though the Axe Vale may be, members yet know that the sky is the limit. For former members include Mary Thomson, winner of Badminton and Olympic team member. Like Natalie, she came from a family with no interest in horses. She started off by riding the vicar's pony, a 14.1 piebald cob which was most unsuitable for the 7 year old girl. Until she was 13 she continued to borrow different ponies, always, Mrs Sleight recalls, remembering to say 'thank you' with suitable enthusiasm, and occasionally simply took a bicycle. Then at last 'my parents gave in' and she was bought a pony of her own. Two years later the partnership went to the Area Horse Trials individually, since there was no Axe Vale team, won and was subsequently placed fourteenth at Stoneleigh, where the Championships were then held.

At the suggestion of Mrs Sleight, she then wrote to Sheila Wilcox, at the time the outstanding woman competitor in horse trials, though Mary Thomson herself knew so little of the national equestrian world that she had never even heard of her. However, after completing her O levels and having sadly sold her pony, she became Sheila Wilcox's working pupil for two and a half years, the perfect start for her future career. During that time she finished her Pony Club exams, passing her A Test, and advises every keen young rider: 'Don't be put off if you don't have your own pony. Go to rallies. You will often be lent one. As you get older and more experienced it becomes more likely.'

Natalie Bucklar, because of the Axe Vale connection, was fortunate enough to do work experience in Mary Thomson's yard: 'It was really good. She took me to one of her Audi Masterclass lectures and she let me ride and watch her school her horses and everything. She helped me know what more serious competitive yards are like. Her Mum's Treasurer of our branch.'

But even Mary Thomson was sometimes in trouble with the DC during Camp. 'I thoroughly enjoyed it, but a group of us girls once got caught in the boys' tent! Then on the Sunday of camp we were all meant to go to church. We would hack over and tie up the ponies outside. My best friend couldn't go because she had broken her leg and it was too long a hack, so I didn't want to go either.'

Somewhat against her better judgment, Mrs Sleight agreed that the two girls should remain behind. When the others had gone, they took their ponies down to the river with only headcollars on, and were splashing about under the bridge. Something frightened the two ponies, who bolted down the road. The two girls followed as best they could, on and on, looking with horror at the skid marks in the tarmac and, even worse, red marks which they were convinced were blood-stains, but eventually turned out to be traces of the red headcollar rope. Finally the girl with the broken leg had to be abandoned, sobbing, on the verge. A man in a car then took pity on the other lone girl. The ponies were eventually traced to the camp of a different branch of the Pony Club some miles away and both girls and ponies were safely back at their own camp before the return of the party from church. However, after a telephone call from the neighbouring DC, Mrs Sleight expressed her views on the girls' behaviour in no uncertain terms.

— 8 —

PONIES

The relationship between child and pony is perhaps the most important thread in the whole structure of the Pony Club. For those children lucky enough to have a pony of their own, having the right pony in size and conformation, in ability, schooling and above all in temperament, is vital. This may well be the first love affair in the child's life: it is essential that the partnership should be well matched. But, unlike the best marriages, however good the match, such partnerships should not last a lifetime, except in the case of an elderly pony. Children outgrow a once-ideal pony, physically and often mentally. Fortunate then are those with younger brothers or sisters awaiting the pony. Otherwise the right home must be found for the pony, where he can show his full potential, as well as the next pony for the rider, who then has the challenge of building up a new relationship.

Choosing a pony is not easy. It is usually wisest to take a knowledgeable adviser when looking and to have the pony vetted before buying it. There is nothing more heartbreaking than the disappointment of a lame pony. Important points to consider when deciding include: the age, size and experience of the rider, what sort of things the rider wishes to do, where the pony is going to live and how much knowledgeable and experienced support there will be for helping the partnership to work. Being safe in traffic is essential for everyone today, if more vital for those whose every ride must include busy roads than for those living in some remote moorland area. Be absolutely honest with yourself about all these issues.

The right pony is particularly important for very young children. The three Dingle sisters in the Thetford Chase branch in Norfolk, Claire, 10, Victoria, eight, and five-year-old Hannah, are fortunate. Claire got her first pony, a Shetland, when she was two, and joined the Pony Club at four. She went straight away to Junior Camp: 'I fell off at least nine times when the pony put his head down.' Star, the 12.2 pony now being ridden by Hannah, was first bought for Claire when she was six. She is, Mrs Dingle says, 'My Nanny, aren't you, dear?' In winter she pulled the sledge, equipped with an old surcingle and two ropes.

Claire now has a delightful coloured pony with a wall eye named Megan, who is that rare combination, a pony prepared to go gently with a tiny child, or take an older child round a cross-country or showjumping course. 'She won't beat the clock but I tell them you don't want that the rest of the time.' Victoria has Zippy.

'He's a boy's pony really, but Victoria rides more like a boy,' says her mother.

Mrs Dingle's own horse is a young one so she does not ride with them but comes on a bicycle, and even Hannah hacks out off a leading rein. 'I need the other two well mounted so that I can help Hannah if necessary. I'm looking forward to the next pony because I'll be able to ride that as well.'

Having the right ponies makes everything else so much simpler. Hannah finds it much easier to learn to ride 'in a hacking situation. The pony's going forward anyway. It gets them going much better. In a riding school situation all you're doing is nagging.'

Mrs Dingle only learnt to ride herself when she was 15, but has been remarkably successful with her family. 'I think I've made mistakes. You put them in situations which you learn not to. Claire went cross-country before she was really ready. With Victoria I've held her back a bit. Claire was not frightened but she was probably not as successful as she should have been. You have to try not to realise your own ambitions, which we are all guilty of to a certain extent. I always try and make certain the pony comes first. Claire knows the pony is not a real winner because it will never shoot round with its head in the air, but, having had one like that for a short time, she's sensible enough to know that's not what she wants. They have as much fun playing round at home with games and their hacks out as they would if you took them out competing. It's amazing how they can amuse themselves with a few cones and buckets and things, left to their own devices. I think they've had enough experience with a few hairy moments to realise what their limitations are.' Mrs Dingle is keen to let them do things for themselves even though they may not do it so well. 'But it does drive you crazy sometimes. You have to walk away don't you?'

She does not believe in encouraging them too much until they are about Hannah's age. This, however, is not how the older two see things. They do not sympathise with the way 'she'll be really keen one minute then half an hour later she won't want to ride ever again' which is so typical of many five-year-olds. 'Hannah's more keen on singing but we don't want to encourage the singing,' say her sisters, disparagingly.

A young competitor at the Cottesmore Pony Club mini gymkhana.
(A. & B. Sorohan: Event Prints)

At Easter, their branch has a cross-country for the older ones and an Easter egg hunt for the younger ones, when they have to get off to collect the eggs, again requiring a sympathetic pony. 'Victoria used to be the best at it. She used to have to share hers out because she got so many,' says Claire, impressed. She herself enjoys rides in Thetford Forest, and says that all her best friends are in the Pony Club. 'They all like the same things as me. They all like ponies. Whereas at school they get a bit bored if you're talking about ponies because there aren't many people who like ponies especially at small schools. The rest are more into pop stuff so I like more of the friendly side of the Pony Club.'

Victoria agrees. 'If there's anyone wandering round on their own they'll soon find a friend.'

Claire remembers how she 'fell off in this dressage test. It wasn't made like a dressage test, they were doing it for experience. It was getting marked. I was cantering a circle on the right rein from C and got round to the other side and the pony wanted to go back to the others that were standing by A and she went that way and I went the other. Then when I got on the saddle slipped round . . .'

Claire, having just passed her C Test, tells how in their branch there is an unofficial E Test for those of Hannah's age. Hannah missed the first day of camp having just had chickenpox. On the second day 'they were all told they would take a test and if they got it they'd get a felt to put under their badge. It sounded great to Hannah. All of a sudden Hannnah didn't feel ill any more. She came next day to take her E Test and all you have to do is know what a hoofpick is and walk and trot without your Mummy leading you. You don't have to be able to rise and I think you have to know what hay is, but even if you get everything wrong you still get the felt.'

Victoria has her D+. One of the others was retaking. 'If you fail a test it's all right really because you know what you failed on so you can brush it up. I failed Road Safety the first time because I was just going out in front of a car when he stopped me. But I've passed it now. Examiners are usually nice.'

The branch's mini tetrathlon, with a maximum age of 11, is held in the Dingle family's field. 'It's a really small, titchy course and it's really friendly. It's not at all competitive. But everyone likes our Tet. People come from Newmarket.'

Claire took Victoria's Zippy to the Pony Club Meet. 'I don't know who the lady was but she was really helpful. I was meant to stay with the DC the whole way round but there were others with her and they were too slow. Zippy's been used to going at the front, and he was with the Master most of the time. The Master said, 'That's fine. You're probably better than me in front.' Zippy was giving them all a lead over big ditches.'

Some of the best ponies are fortunate ever to have the chance to show their worth. Laura Carbutt (11) of the Essex and Suffolk Hunt branch, described her pony, Barley, in the branch newsletter. 'Barley had a very bad start to life, he was herded into a cattle truck off the Welsh hills and they used string round his

Samantha and Ben Buckley with Pip Squeak. *(Rita Buckley)*

ears to pull him up the ramp, he was very badly treated, that is why he hates men and is head shy. He was taken to Colchester market to be sold for dog meat but luckily someone loved his colour and bought him for £5. He had a very happy home for about seventeen years and then he was given to me.

'I have done everything on him from gymkhana to showjumping, Working Hunter pony and lots of Pony Club. He has taught me everything I know about riding and sadly now it is time for me to go onto a bigger pony. I shall miss him dreadfully but he still has a busy life teaching disabled children to ride; there will never be another pony like Barley.'

Riding for the Disabled is something at which many of the smaller Pony Club ponies excel. Pip Squeak, a 12 hands pony now aged 23, belongs to the Buckley family in the Oakley West branch. When the Princess Royal visited his Riding for the Disabled group at Christmas time, it was his responsibility to carry the Virgin Mary in the mounted Nativity play. He disgraced himself by stopping immediately in front of the distinguished visitor for an extended 'call of nature', to the embarrassment of his owner and amusement of the Princess.

Pip Squeak is still taking part in Pony Club activities with Ben Buckley (9) and Samantha (6). Like many such wise ponies, he keeps the older rider firmly in his place, depositing him on the floor at any hint of over confidence, whilst encouraging the younger sister, for whom he recently won second prize in a Working Hunter Pony class. Although Samantha first went to mini camp and actually slept in a tent at the age of four with the Bedfordshire South branch to which they then belonged, her successful day in the ring was the first occasion on which she had jumped a fence.

Some of the best ponies spend more years in the Pony Club than any child will ever do. When Clare Eeley of the Bicester in Oxfordshire took her pony to stay with her grandmother in Brecon and attended camp there, one of the instructresses, aged around 25, told Clare that at her age she had had a pony very like Clare's named Tinker. Even when Clare said that was her pony's name, neither realised that it was indeed the same Tinker, until her grandmother explained how she had found the pony.

The coloured pony which Clare's older sister Jo is riding in the photograph originally belonged to their mother. She was bought for her out of the local grocer's shop as a three-year-old when Mrs Eeley was 12: 'The last thing you should ever do.' But they took it very slowly and Melody became the classic Pony Club pony. She eventually represented different branches of the Pony Club at Area level in every one of the disciplines: Dressage, Showjumping, Horse Trials, Polo and the Prince Philip Cup, reaching the Zone finals. She was also a top class

Jo Eeley aged 12 on Melody aged 27. *(Sue Eeley)*

Working Hunter Pony and competed in the Hickstead Showjumping. At the end of her life she competed in horse trials for Jo when she was 12 and Jo's brother Ben played polo on her.

Mrs Eeley, herself an experienced instructress, is a great believer in 'keeping the outgrown pony whilst introducing the next stage so that if ever there's a crisis you can go back. The older or smaller one may be more suitable for hunting, for example. If you're almost over-horsing them then you have to be so careful because the most important thing I'm convinced is confidence with either the rider or the horse and once you've lost that you might as well give up.'

An experienced, knowledgeable family can take on a pony which would not be suitable for the Pony Club member herself unaided. Fourteen-year-old Jo is lucky enough to have a mother who is an instructress and a father who passed his own Pony Club A Test (thereby setting a challenge for Jo: 'I can't let Dad beat me!'). Her mother in any case likes bringing on young horses and 'we try to find the ones other people don't want'. She considers 'the most worrying trend in the Pony Club is the amount of money going into the animals which therefore makes the whole thing much more serious. Even if you do have a lot of money to spend on a horse it doesn't guarantee the combination of horse and rider will be successful. When buying youngsters and bringing them on, the partnership has time to develop together, with Pony Club activities being ideal opportunities for this learning process. It also takes a lot of luck. It might go lame, but that's why a lot of us do it: you can't predict what's going to happen. I'm sure it's good for children, character building.'

The pony they now found for Jo was indeed character building. At first she was 'basically unrideable. You couldn't touch her at the beginning. She'd fly to the back of her stable.' She looked dreadful, had white marks on her head from some earlier trauma and 'appeared to have a personality problem not apparent at the time of purchase!' It later emerged that she had barely been broken in. They had either to persevere or shoot her.

The mare was not then suitable for Jo to ride, but her father rode her for long hours at a time, sitting quietly whilst the pony turned herself inside out. It is still early days, but the pony is beginning to show exceptional talent, and Jo is now competing on her. Such experiments are not for most families, and certainly not for members without the necessary back-up. But if the pony eventually follows in the footsteps of such illustrious predecessors as Melody, the Eeley family will have cause for considerable satisfaction.

Every reliable schoolmaster pony had once to be schooled. For Jo, Melody was the perfect pony who knew everything. For her mother at the same age, Melody was the unbroken three-year-old. The satisfaction of making a young horse is undeniable, but it is not a task to be undertaken without knowledgeable and experienced support. There is too much at stake for both the rider and the pony.

— 9 —

SHOWJUMPING

Away from the Pony Club, the world of showjumping is quite separate from that of horse trials or of pure dressage, despite the tendency of the popular press to refer to leading horse trials riders as 'show jumpers'. The position is different in the Pony Club, where there are close links between showjumping, horse trials, dressage and even tetrathlon. The same members often represent their branch at Area level in more than one of these disciplines. Some members do concentrate exclusively on showjumping, but they are a minority.

Whilst many branches run their own showjumping competitions, these are often combined with dressage classes, thus helping the young showjumping enthusiast to appreciate the need to improve his or her flat work and through this the jumping. But there is considerable scope for taking part in showjumping competitions in the Pony Club, particularly as a member of a team. Many branches hold unofficial inter-branch showjumping competitions for local teams of every age. Sometimes the class divisions are based on the pony's size and sometimes on the rider's age.

In addition to the Inter Branch Area competitions which culminate in the Showjumping Championships at Weston Park, there is also a second comparable national team competition, with different rules, with the Final at Hickstead. Many regions also have local competitions for Pony Club branch teams. Amongst the most famous is that held on the first day of the Burghley Three-Day event for branches by invitation only from the Midlands and East Anglia. Several Areas have special inter-branch team competitions, perhaps established in memory of some well-known local personality, each with its own rules, but these frequently include a showjumping element.

Charlotte Barker of the Bedale branch in Yorkshire was 16 in 1991 when she and her mare Crisp were asked at relatively short notice to fill a place in the Inter-Branch Showjumping team for the Area competition. Charlotte was already in the Horse Trials and Dressage teams, and at the time it was branch policy to avoid having members in all three teams. However, with lameness and other difficulties, two substitutes were needed. Despite her enthusiasm for horse trials, Charlotte has never qualified for those Championships at Weston Park: the top two individuals qualify and she has been third on several occasions. 'It was a great shock to everyone there' when the showjumping team succeeded in qualifying immediately.

Expectations for the Championships were not running high. Although one of the team members, Fiona Chapman, is a very experienced showjumper, the branch had not had a high success record, and had often not entered a team at all. The other two team members were sisters, Abigail and Lucinda Broad, but, although Charlotte had been in a horse trials team with them, they had not been in a showjumping team together. Even when they set off for Weston Park, 'No-one down there expected us to do any good and neither did we.' Yet from this inauspicious start they found that a showjumping team has a magic of its own: 'It was amazing how there was a lot of team spirit between us. It was difficult; we didn't even know one of the members but the way it works, a bit like a Nations Cup, it builds a lot of team spirit and everyone's working out the scores and you know we're really doing quite well actually. Being in a team is very nerve wracking: there isn't any individual placing and if you make a mistake that's everybody out of it. We all sat there looking very ill and very sick beforehand. Then it was really good. With the eventing, when you find out how you've done

Charlotte Barker and Crisp at the Show Jumping Championships at Weston Park 1992. *(Pleasure Prints, Crookham Common)*

you're not on your horse any more, but with showjumping we'd just done the jump off and another team that we know well had just arrived to do the horse trials next day so there were a lot of us around. We were expecting not to have done too well ...' The excitement when they realised that they had won the Showjumping Championships was immense.

Sadly, such moments do not last for ever. A year later, the same Bedale team were no longer outsiders but reigning Champions and hot favourites. In the first round, all four were clear. 'The commentators kept going on about 'no-one's ever won it two years running' and especially when we'd set off so well in the first round they were getting more and more excited.' But it was not to be: only one of the four was clear in the second round.

Charlotte's older sister, Emma, is as keen and capable a rider as Charlotte, so that most of Charlotte's ponies were passed on to her as Emma outgrew them. However when Charlotte was 13, Emma's horse had unfortunately to be put down because of a heart problem, so that Charlotte had to find a new horse. It was a long time before they found Crisp, and 'she wasn't really what Mum wanted: only five, a mare and she hadn't really been taught to jump. I fell off her all the time when I first got her because she thought so much more quickly than I did.' Much work was needed for Charlotte and Crisp to reach Championship standard, but neither of the Barker sisters are afraid of hard work. Charlotte at 18 has combined her A-level work with passing her Pony Club H Test. She is now doing some teaching in the Pony Club and working towards her A Test. Emma has already achieved the rare distinction of passing her A Test and is now doing medicine. Winning the Pony Club Championships, passing the A Test and becoming a doctor are all rare achievements. The Barker sisters have already achieved two of these feats, and look set to increase their total.

A competitor at the Show Jumping Championships in 1991. *(Bob Langrish)*

10

RALLIES AND FUN, MOUNTED AND UNMOUNTED

'The Working Rally is the backbone of the Club,' declares the Pony Club *Year Book*, and defines a working rally as one at which instruction is given, which may be mounted or dismounted. Some members regard rallies as a chore, and go only because it is necessary to attend at least three in a year to be eligible to compete in Area teams. Wiser members, and their parents, see rallies as exceptional value: there is not usually a charge for attending, unless the facilities, indoor school or cross-country course, for example, have had to be hired. The regular provision of free or cheap riding and stable management lessons alone makes the Pony Club subscription good value. Properly run, rallies can be much more than that.

'Absolutely brilliant,' is how Camilla Fraser, who, at 19, has just given up being a member of the Warwickshire, remembers them. 'All my same lot of friends were there. I used to go every two weeks or so. Being at boarding school I was quite envious when people said they were at rallies and I was stuck at school. They were in lovely places with wonderful jumps – Charlecote Park was always a great favourite – and once there was this river and we all took off our saddles and went swimming which was great and I'd never done it before.' During the day they would enjoy a leisurely picnic lunch and chat together, as well as alternating use of the show jumps and cross-country fences, 'a bit of stable management and swapping of ponies.' This was particularly popular: each member would afterwards be asked to describe the different horses and ponies, and it was satisfying when other people wanted to ride your horse.

Camilla feels that she learnt a fair amount, particularly when the lesson was specific to what she needed, but she really remembers rallies for 'just being there with your friends and having a laugh.' Her same group stayed together throughout their Pony Club careers, despite brief interludes when someone moved in front of or behind their contemporaries on the test ladder. 'To begin with there were a lot of us, but then a lot of my friends gave up. I carried on for another couple of years and then it becomes rather dull when none of your friends are doing it. But then when Emma (her younger sister) is doing it I miss it! Rallies were just having fun basically which I think is very important.'

Jo Eeley too, who is 14, finds Bicester rallies great fun. 'The Chief Instructor is good and we do quite a lot of jumping.' She also enjoys going along to help at mini rallies for the under eights. One enormously popular event in the Bicester is the Long Distance Ride, which lasts for three days in the summer holidays. The object is to cover a total of 75 miles, though on one occasion an error in measuring meant that they were doing over 30 miles a day. Suitable farms are found for the group, which may total 20 to 25, to stay at, with children sleeping in a barn in sleeping bags, adults in a caravan and ponies turned out in a field.

Mrs Jenny Dixey, DC of the Whaddon Chase, is a great believer in combining the teaching of the basics (to parents as well as children when possible) with making everything enjoyable. Her rallies are enlivened in many different ways: gymkhana games, long rides through the woods, treasure hunts, exchanging ponies and bareback riding. She hopes as many activities as possible will be 'fun for the family, a great ice breaker. Lots of parents still think its very snobby, but children can help parents and parents can help children.' She likes to see more stable management evenings including parents, many of whom do not know the basics. She feels that the competitive children with knowledgeable parents will manage without much help, and identifies with the others. 'If you've not had it easy yourself you actually know what it is to struggle. My parents weren't horse-minded at all. I can remember now changing in the back of the car after school and then having quite a long drive back home afterwards. It's amazing, as a child if you are really keen on something you'll put up with anything.'

She is adamant that 'Any child at whatever standard can have a huge amount of fun' and has always encouraged even children without ponies to join, persuading the others to take turns with them. Taking part in a team quiz, with regular evening practices, gives children without ponies a chance to compete on equal terms and to build up team spirit, and if there are transport difficulties a roster can be worked out. 'It's an interest that doesn't involve them going into the cities.' The production of a pantomime 'gave everybody the opportunity to do something and see each other as a branch'. However the demands this made on the organisers were such that even the indefatigable Mrs Dixey gave up the pantomime after two years.

The Axe Vale in Devon is a branch which specialises in all kinds of activities, entertaining as well as instructional, mounted and unmounted. There are non-competitive rides round small courses and Easter Egg hunts. They also compete successfully in inter-branch stable management competitions. Natalie Bucklar has enjoyed all these, and through them has built up the confidence to start eventing and to persist with her B Test despite an initial setback. Much of this is because of the personality of the DC: 'Mrs Sleight keeps people in order; you daren't do anything that might put her out. She is quite fierce but friendly at the same time. She always encourages you to do things. We all fit in: everybody helps each other and the older ones show the younger ones "If you plait like this

Trotting Poles. *(Bob Langrish)*

it looks better".' Clearly the system works: Nicky Bernard-Hayklan has just passed her A Test at the first attempt.

Mrs Sleight also leads the branch in some enterprising ventures. Camp, instead of always being held locally, has been held in Exmoor, Dartmoor and the New Forest, with lorries laid on to ease the transport difficulties. Axe Vale visits to foreign countries have become legendary and are described in another chapter. Chrissy Howick, who in common with several of her friends still belongs at 21, feels that the atmosphere is special: 'You've just got to join in and get on. People from all sorts of different types of schools and different areas of the country all muck in with everything. It's taught me a lot. She expects you to want to do it and be enthusiastic. She'll quite often enter you for a test so you haven't much choice, but only when she knows you're ready.' Members are expected to be self-reliant: 'We've stayed in some funny places for camp; some of us are quite good at making makeshift stables.' Whilst younger members can find their DC quite frightening at first, they 'soon get to know'. Chrissy recalls how her pony used to buck her off all the time 'and I remember Mrs Sleight leading me round for hours and hours and hours. She's done that for a lot of people, not just for camp; afterwards she'll go to the houses and help them there.' Mrs Sleight has also inspired the branch recently to raise money for 'Riders for Romania', the

Axe Vale members cleaning Bicton Arena Stables to raise money for the Eventers Romanian Appeal. *(Mrs Sleight)*

charitable group of event riders, including Mary Thomson, who are working to help Romanian orphanages.

The branch has a most entertaining magazine filled with tales of the past year, delightful Christmas stories, branch news, quizzes and sometimes articles by such former members as Mary Thomson and her head groom Annie Collings. Another branch with an excellent magazine is the South Pool, also in Devon. This includes a number of articles on serious topics, written by vets and instructors. South Pool members appreciate long, organised rides in the superb country which they are lucky enough to have access to, undeterred by harsh weather conditions. Forty-two riders enjoyed a ride round a large estate despite

PLATE FIVE *(above)* Relaxing with a friend *(Iain Burns)*, and *(below)* The ring at Hickstead during the final of the Pony Club Show Jumping *(Iain Burns)*

PLATE SIX   *(above)* Four members of the Cotley branch *(Iain Burns)*, and *(below)* Wormwood Scrubs Branch (see page 66) *(one of a set of postcards for the Branch by Francis Blake)*

pouring rain, and Eleanor Baker, who is eight, clearly loved the excitement of the Moorland Ride across Dartmoor, despite appalling conditions: 'There were steep hills to ride up and down and lots of streams to cross. One pony fell in a bog but managed to get out again. There were hailstones and my face was hurting with the cold. You wouldn't be able to get back on your own because it was too foggy and you would get lost so we all had to stay together. I got very wet but it was one of my best days riding and I can't wait to go next time.'

For most branches, the year's programme will include, in addition to the various competitive fixtures, the more traditional working rallies; at least one and preferably more mounted expeditions, rides or treasure hunts; and a number of unmounted outings. As well as stable management rallies and more light hearted gatherings within the branch itself, there will usually be visits to places of interest. The relatively small (just 73 members) Llangibby branch in Wales included in their programme for a single year, as well as shows, hunter trials and Camp, visits to the Avon and Somerset Mounted Police, Olympia, Badminton and the Hunt Kennels, in addition to a mock hunt, a tetrathlon and other competitions. Other branches find that members have too many other commitments for such a wealth of opportunities to receive adequate support, and concentrate on a single popular venture. The range of activities open to members is enormous: if a particular branch is not currently offering what its members would like, suggestions are usually appreciated, especially if someone is available to complete the organisation, provided that there is likely to be sufficient support to make it worth while.

11

IN THE CITY

Pony Club in the city may seem a contradiction in terms. Yet there are a number of flourishing inner city branches offering chances for children from every conceivable background who live miles from the country to ride, learn about horses and ponies, go to Pony Club camp, take tests and join in Pony Club activities with members from other branches.

Most of these branches are based on a single centre. Whilst they are often inspired by an outstanding individual, the spirit engendered between members, helpers, instructors, parents and friends is something very special. Few of those who pass the gates of Wormwood Scrubs prison will have any conception of what lies behind the gloomy buildings. Even playing fields and some common land do little to prepare the visitor for the shock of rounding a corner to find, incongruously, a group of ponies and children having a riding lesson.

Wormwood Scrubs became a branch of the Pony Club in 1992 with Sister Mary Joy Langdon as District Commissioner. Sister Mary Joy was a member of the Pony Club herself as a child, and has ridden all her life. A religious Sister of the Infant Jesus, she came to Wormwood Scrubs to help with Riding for the Disabled, but found that such scant organisation as then existed was about to collapse completely. She then decided to start creating something from this feeble base, though there were no buildings, just 'three little Shetland ponies which were here'. She bought two of them and the third was on loan and has never been reclaimed. From these beginnings the Pony Centre grew fast. Sister Mary Joy remembers her astonishment at having 25 children on a Saturday. Today it is around 100 with a waiting list filling half an exercise book.

Since there are only fourteen horses and ponies, much of the time at the Pony Centre is not spent actually riding, but in helping and learning, and in caring for all the other animals, the dogs, puppies, goats, kittens, rabbits and guinea pigs: 'They just have to learn to respect animals.' Many children and adults ride at the Centre under the Riding for the Disabled Association (the RDA). As Sister Mary Joy says, 'I have children from all walks of life here. You name it, they come here. A lot of people with special needs, vast numbers of youngsters, and the ponies can do something for them: very therapeutic. I've got young people working here that wouldn't get on anywhere else.'

When the Centre was first started, there were no stables and vandalism was a constant anxiety. This threat has receded with better security and improved relations. In the early days tack was stolen and gypsies tried to steal the ponies. On Christmas Eve the ponies had to spend the night in the girls' changing room at the nearby sports stadium. 'Gypsies had camped up here and every time you turned your back or went away they were over here.' So they piled hay on the ground and filled all the waste paper baskets up with water. Since then, an alarm system has been installed, ponies freeze marked, stables, a tack room and a lecture room built with voluntary labour and plans have now been put in for an indoor riding school. 'If we get the planning permission, we'll get the money,' Sister Mary Joy declares confidently.

Once the Centre became an approved British Horse Society riding school, the next stage was to become a branch of the Pony Club. Most children who ride at weekends are members: in cases of need help may sometimes be found for subscriptions. As soon as the branch was formed, they held their first Camp, in two big tents, one of them donated by London Electricity. 'Thirty-eight youngsters came, the weather was hot, the games fun, the ponies brilliant, the teams were great, the food delicious (thanks to the volunteers), sleep, or lack of it, not so good, but roll on next camp.' Members are all immaculately turned out in matching scarlet sweat shirts and scarlet silks on their hats.

A team from the branch competed in the Area Quiz competition, and, most impressively, came second, only being beaten on the hunting, racing and polo questions. The need to take turns in actually riding pays dividends in time available for learning theory, which is taught in a most imaginative way, and is of great value when members take Pony Club tests. Next, 'We took two teams to Bedford for the Area Prince Philip Cup. We came last in every race but we actually came second in the tack and turnout. As I said to the children, our ponies had done five hours' work out in the school on the Saturday. They're very versatile because a lot of our work is RDA work. We've put our mark on the Pony Club events we have been to.'

There is also a thriving vaulting group in the branch, a wide-ranging Fun Day at Easter and some activities which are not available to country branches. The tiny Shetland won first prize in the London Harness Parade, Horseman's Sunday is a memorable occasion and they were given a box at Olympia. Perhaps Anthony Joyce, who comes to the Centre under RDA, summmed it up best: 'Besides riding, I am allowed to do everything – fill the hay nets, clean the tack and even answer the phone. I get help when I need it and nobody hurries me ... There are lots of lovely people as well (as ponies) at the Pony Centre, but to me Sister Mary Joy is the loveliest of them all.'

At the other end of London, in Docklands, there is an equally remarkable branch. Few people, driving beneath the arches of a former flyover, would dream that there was a horse or pony within miles, unless they happened to notice the horse box parked there. Yet actually within the arched structure itself, replacing a former warehouse, is stabling for 16 horses and ponies, and an indoor school as well, albeit one shaped, in the words of its creator, 'like a banana'. This remarkable establishment is the brainchild of Miss Lydia Greaves, now District Commissioner of the Docklands branch of the Pony Club.

Miss Greaves was born close by and has always had a great love of horses although her parents could never afford riding for her. In 1970 she resolved to do something to help local girls in a similar predicament. With the help of two friends she built stabling for 12 horses which has since been extended to 16. The Newham Riding School and Association is now a registered charity with one paid employee and three trainees on a 'springboard' scheme. The three trainees have now completed their BHS Stage 2 exams and are working towards their Stage 3. The school is British Horse Society approved and, because of its charitable status and grants which it receives, pupils pay just £3 an hour compared with a going rate of around £20 elsewhere. New premises are currently being built close to the ski slope on the A13, not far away; Miss Greaves is looking forward with delight to the move, though she is also conscious of the warning of the Princess Royal, when she visited the Riding for the Disabled Group there, about the need to keep the present marvellous atmosphere.

When Dennis Colton, National Inspector of riding schools for the BHS, originally put forward the suggestion that she should form a branch of the Pony Club, Miss Greaves was adamant: 'No way did I ever want to.' She could see no future in it and felt that the Pony Club had the wrong image. But after further discussions she finally agreed. 'I've changed my mind. They've made us very welcome and I must say I've found some nice, helpful, really, really kind people.' During 1993, although Miss Greaves feels that she has not been as active as usual because of the time demanded by the plans for the new equestrian centre, 'the Pony Club has been absolutely brilliant'. It has motivated her team 'to do more for the kids. They all say "When are we doing the next thing?"' The girls, all of whom Miss Greaves describes as 'disadvantaged in some way', are keen to take tests. All have now got D and some C. An outside examiner is always brought in, even for D Test, since the girls are then forced to express their answers coherently, in itself a valuable contribution to their education. Miss Greaves recently took them to a Chinese restaurant to thank them for all their unpaid help. This also was a new and valuable experience for the vast majority.

The girls (there are around 33 members, and all are currently girls) enjoyed camp this year when the ponies were boxed out to Chigwell and members shared a marquee. They have lectures, demonstrations and talks right through the year, and a gymkhana day with rosettes on the green. Branch sweatshirts incorporate a silhouette of cranes at the docks as well as the name: whilst the girls share everything including their clothes, they do 'try to be smart and just a little bit different'. A team competed against four other teams recently in a Quiz night, and emerged victorious. The large group of followers accompanying the team was evidence of the strong local support for the branch.

Members of the Docklands Branch.

There is an excellent committee, made up of skilled professional men and women all giving their time voluntarily. June Redgewell, Assistant DC, and Chief Instructress, is a civil servant who chooses to start work at 6.30 a.m. to enable her to teach later. Miss Greaves, who was practising 'integration' before the word became fashionable, ('If you can't accept being with disabled people, go! It was not pioneering but necessity') is scornful of forms couched in politically correct language asking for statistics about ethnic origins. She and her Treasurer, who comes from Guyana, ignore them. It is a brave official who pursues the issue further with Miss Greaves, who has been described as 'formidable'. Everybody is welcome regardless of religion, colour or politics, provided that they can ride, enjoy themselves and learn. Pony Club members are frequently involved with helping disabled children. For some girls, their time with Miss Greaves has influenced their whole lives. Karen Wheatley is profoundly deaf but is gradually working her way through the BHS exams. 'The difference it has made to her whole life is unbelievable.' Four former girls are now working full-time with horses.

Helping in the yard is regarded as a privilege which has to be earned. Those who are selected to stay behind can justly feel that they have achieved something. A high standard is expected: every time they have taken part in the Riding Horse Parade they have won, and, again through Dennis Colton, ponies from the school were invited to take part in a demonstration at Olympia, giving the girls a chance to warm them up there beforehand, although they were not riding them in the show. A number of the horses have had distinguished pasts, including a successful trotter, an equally successful Welsh cob, and the thirty-year-old Archer, who has appeared in numerous films. If anyone asks for the horses or ponies to appear at anything locally, Miss Greaves tries hard to help. She has done so much for the district, formally through the school and through other positions which she holds, such as Equine Consultant to the London Docklands Development Board, and on an informal basis too. The problem of vandalism is reduced by her standing and contacts: when she started in 1970, there were many facilities for local boys but none at all for the girls. Yet she feels too that she has herself had many opportunities through horses, including travelling in the United States and Canada for Driving for the Disabled, which she is anxious to repay. Docklands in general and particularly its horses and the girls of its Pony Club are the beneficiaries.

Other city branches are in more prosperous areas. Ross Nye, DC of the Hyde Park branch, was honoured in 1988 to be asked, again through Dennis Colton, to form the first official branch of the Pony Club based on a commercial riding stable. An Australian who first came to England nearly 30 years ago with his wife, a leading concert pianist, he found a tiny stable in a Mews close to Hyde Park and set up his riding school. His daughter Kirsty, then a small baby, now runs it with him, and almost all the regular riders of suitable age, about 45 of them, are now Pony Club members. His original stable has been demolished, but he now has stabling for 16 horses in Bathurst Mews with a flat above for Kirsty, so that there is always someone close to the horses, particularly important since they are in stalls not loose boxes because of the confined space. The city life causes other difficulties: parking the horse box in the day time should it be needed is a major problem, and removal of muck is an expensive business.

Mr Nye himself lives near Guildford, and during the Easter and summer holidays the ponies are moved down there, with children staying for a week at a time. Riding holidays take place there, similar to Pony Club Camp, and are very popular, competitive and educational. The final week is known as Senior Week and culminates in a One-Day Event on the final day, particularly special to children whose jumping is usually limited to the logs and puddles of Hyde Park with a turn in the manège there once a fortnight. They revel in dressing smartly for the dressage and showjumping, and striving to emulate the colours of our leading international riders for the cross-country phase. This year camp also included talks and demonstrations by a successful event rider, by a vet on acupuncture and by experts on both showjumping and dressage. Members do not sleep under canvas but in comfort in the attic of Mr and Mrs Nye's home.

With a small river and a lake outside there is plenty of scope for such traditional camp activities as pushing people in.

None of the members own their own ponies. For rallies they have still to pay for the hire of the pony but the tuition is provided free. Because they are expected always to vary the pony they ride and are not allowed to choose a favourite and stick to it, their riding is improved by the wider experience. Whilst most of the original ponies were bought by Mr Nye, he is sometimes now asked to take an outgrown pony so that it will have a good home and useful life. He also operates four RDA groups from his yard.

Riding different ponies is popular with members. Emma Sharpe considers it an advantage of membership to have joint rallies with other branches and exchange ponies with them. Emma is 16 and has been coming regularly since she was nine, although in the last year she has had little time for riding because of her GCSE work: Mr Nye, like Emma herself, is adamant that 'education comes before the riding'. With a lull before the A-level pressure starts to build up, she again helps at the stables every Sunday from 7 a.m. till 5.30 p.m. Such regular helpers are often rewarded with a 'stable ride'. Members all work towards their D, Riding and Road Safety and C Tests. Joanna Rotherham, who is 15, and Vicky de Polo, who is a year younger, have both just passed their C Tests, Joanna in such style that the examiner regretted there was no special credit she could be given.

Many of the members have been riding at the school for a long time: Anoushka Lee first came when she was eight and is now 17. Their parents, by spending their money on regular lessons rather than a pony of their own, are ensuring that the children are well taught and properly supervised at all times: Mr Nye is extremely safety conscious and insisted on hard hats long before this was universally accepted. This safety training stood nine-year-old Tamara Eccleston in good stead recently when she was riding whilst travelling abroad and did fall on her head but was fortunately wearing her crash hat. Like every other branch, they have their particular annual highlights, which include Horseman's Sunday, when there is a draw to see who actually rides during the service, and a coach trip to Badminton cross-country day.

In branches such as these London ones nobody has a pony of their own. It is perhaps more difficult for those without a pony to belong to a branch where most members have one. Philippa has never had a pony, although she first joined the Stanmore branch in Middlesex when she was nine and is leaving now only because she is above the age limit. Yet she says 'I think I've benefitted as much from the Pony Club as my friends who have ponies.' She first joined because the riding school where she was having lessons was used for rallies by the branch. The five friends who joined with her soon gave up, but Philippa showed more determination. She found the competitions exciting, although she declares that

'To begin with, I never came anywhere' and on rally days she really felt that the pony was almost her own.

She particularly enjoyed the stable management side which she would never have learnt without the Pony Club. Despite failing her C Test the first time, she persisted and later passed her C+ as well. Indeed Philippa now plans, when she has finished at college, to return to the riding stables and take her BHS exams. When event and rally dates were known she would book her favourite pony for fixtures at the riding school. Otherwise she went on her feet 'and often they'd let me borrow their ponies'. She feels that her riding benefitted from riding such a wide range of different ponies. There were also numerous unmounted rallies and games.

Soon Philippa was involved with the tetrathlon, having first become interested in triathlons, omitting the mounted phase, and sometimes travelling long distances to compete. So enthusiastic has she become that she has actually started a pentathlon group at her college.

Philippa considers that there is a positive side: she has always been aware of how much time a pony takes and not having one has enabled her to pursue a much wider range of interests. Although she never went to camp, she went to Guide camp instead. Despite the drawbacks, she feels that 'Pony Club fulfilled all the things that I wanted to do'.

Philippa proves that the Pony Club is worthwhile even if there is no prospect of ever having a pony of your own. Even those who live in areas where they never see a blade of grass should not give up hope: there may well be a branch of the Pony Club close at hand, waiting to help.

12

AGAINST THE ODDS

The inner city and suburban branches do face major problems which never confront those lucky enough to live in open country. However, for some branches, the problem is not lack of space but the opposite. Members of the Ross-shire branch may find themselves travelling as far for one of their own branch functions as members elsewhere travel for the furthest Area competition. Although most members live near the East coast, one family lives at Durness on the extreme north-west coast of Scotland and another at Achiltibuie in a remote spot on the West coast. Despite this, and the consequently high cost of obtaining good instructors, the branch holds three camps at different times in the year and monthly rallies, which in winter are dismounted as they do not have the use of an indoor school. All the same, the branch regularly sends teams to compete at Area level in most of the disciplines. Even for the Quiz team, travelling without horses, this can involve a long journey: a recent competition at Stornoway necessitated a four hour ferry crossing.

Occasionally all four team members have come from a single family, the Greenwood family. In 1990 Oliver Greenwood at fifteen qualified for the Championships in both Horse Trials and Tetrathlon, whilst his sister qualified the same horse for the Riding Clubs Championships. Even for them, the journey seemed a long one in their ancient horse box, but Oliver felt it was worthwhile when he was 'best boy' in his Arena at Weston Park. Despite the scarcity of opportunities for competing in tetrathlons, Oliver has persisted with such determination that he is now ranked eleventh in the United Kingdom. In 1992 he struggled to combine the Tetrathlon Championships at Stoneleigh, the team Showjumping Championships at Weston Park and the BHS Three-day event at Blair Castle all within ten days.

For some boys, membership of the Pony Club in itself may appear to be a battle against the odds, for in a few branches boys are a tiny minority of members. This has never worried 15-year-old Marty Fields of the Spooners and West Dartmoor, although the secretary describes him as 'almost the lone boy in a wilderness of girls in this branch'. He first started riding at a riding school when he was six, then his mother bought a pony for him and his older sister Pip to share. They shared a field belonging to Kate Allenby, a near neighbour. Marty has wonderful riding country right up to his door and, as his mother says, 'If they see a rider in the distance it's generally somebody they know.' Most rallies are within hacking distance. When necessary the DC, who is in the haulage business, can usually lay on a lorry for all those without transport to share. 'It's a really friendly Pony Club. If you forget something at an event, someone will always lend you it. Someone once even forgot a bridle.' Marty is sympathetic: he himself has been known on occasions to go for a ride with the reins crossed beneath the pony's neck. Perhaps this is an indication of the confidence he had in his original pony, which he only recently sold. The wide open spaces of the moor are dangerously alluring to many horses and ponies.

When Marty first joined, there was one other boy attending regularly, but he left a year later. There have usually been a few others belonging since then, but 'I was the only one actively going round all the events.' He was soon involved in tetrathlon, and in the Prince Philip Cup. For his final year in the Prince Philip Cup he was team captain and the team won the Area and got to the Zone, but 'our Area doesn't seem to be the quality of the rest,' Marty says modestly. Now that he is too old he is helping to train the team. He has competed in the Area tetrathlon twice, coming 3rd and 6th. Despite the appeal of tetrathlon to boys, boys' and girls' teams being separate is a disadvantage: he has usually had to compete as an individual. Belonging to 'a team of two with Simon who doesn't ride!' was not altogether satisfactory.

For camp again he is often the only boy, but this does not concern him at all. 'Camp is very good – I love camp,' he says. 'Sometimes being on your own at nights means that you go to bed earlier and the next day you're awake when the others are tired. During the day it doesn't make much difference.' The other members have cause to be grateful to Marty, for together with his father he has put in much work on the cross-country course. He is also always in demand for such tasks as setting up the show jumps.

He and his sister get on well together. If their mother complains that Marty shows less enthusiasm than Pip for looking after his horse and cleaning the tack, she is also well aware of the help he is often able to give Pip at camp or on Pony Club outings which she needs because she is diabetic. The two work well together on their riding, offering each other constructive criticism. Marty has been unfortunate in belonging to a branch with so few other active boys, but he has had the sense to appreciate that this does not matter at all. 'I'm enjoying riding more than I've ever done before with the young pony to bring on,' he says.

For other members, the physical problems with which they have to contend make membership of the Pony Club in itself a remarkable achievement. Pippa Langston, who belongs to the same branch as Marty, is 17. She looks after her own pony, hacks out on Dartmoor, goes hunting and has captained the Junior Mounted Games team for the branch, regularly attended camp (the first year she won the Most Improved Rider), passed her C+ Test, ridden in showjumping teams, won two dressage cups at the annual Pony Club show and was a member of the Dressage team which came third at the Area, apart from working for three

Pippa Langston on Torfee, who is also carrying the oxygen cylinders, at a show in May 1990, just before her transplant. *(D. H. Roberts, Ultra Image, Plymouth)*

A-levels. At the local show she has won the Working Hunter Pony Championship and, another year, both the Working Hunter Pony class and the Best Rider. At the last count her rosettes numbered 512. She was also born with cystic fibrosis and three years ago had a heart and lung transplant operation.

Pippa continued riding right up to the transplant, although afterwards she was not supposed to ride for six months. The doctors, unused to horses, declared that she could ride provided she did not fall off. A compromise was reached and she did not jump or gallop. In the year leading up to the operation, she was unable to ride without oxygen. Oxygen cylinders are extremely heavy. Her pony Torfee learnt to carry the cylinders, and can be seen with them in the photograph. The picture has since been borrowed by doctors to demonstrate what can be done despite cystic fibrosis. For camp, friends learnt to do her physiotherapy for her and, as camp was then up on the moors far from water or electricity, she had to go to the nearest hotel twice daily to use the breathing machine, returning to sleep in the barn.

For her work experience, Pippa's godfather arranged for her to take her own horse with her and work in the stable yard at Badminton for two and a half weeks under the Duke of Beaufort's stud groom. She was there at the same time as the British Horse Trials team in training for the Olympics. 'Ian Stark's dog kept trying to chew our tack!' She also has a special relationship with Desert Orchid, whom she visits regularly. She had a Get Well card from him in hospital after her operation. When she visited the Horse of the Year Show, a preliminary letter to enquire about facilities for using her nebuliser resulted in a free ticket, a pass to go everywhere and being taken backstage to see all the horses.

For Cystic Fibrosis Raceday at Doncaster, Pippa was interviewed on television by John Francome. At the time she was thinking of being a jockey, and he kindly arranged for her to ride in a Ladies' Race at Doncaster, but unfortunately she has had some rejection since the transplant and her lungs are not as good as they were so that this was not possible.

When Pippa was very ill before she had the transplant, they selected the Barcelona Olympics as the goal to aim at, and got there. 'Richard Walker stopped right in front of me, and we met Matt Ryan just before the Olympics not knowing who he was. We were there when Christie won the 100 metres and also when Nick Skelton had his disaster. It was a lovely experience to go, a sort of celebration of the transplant.'

Pippa's horses have to learn a new style of going cross-country. They jump, stop for Pippa to get her breath back, go on and jump the next fence. But at camp she joins in on equal terms. 'This year I won the Dressage, but I had a fence down in the jumping. There are the traditional water fights and hay fights. Any food we didn't like we chucked over our heads into the hay bales. People in the toilets in a horse box were pushed down the hill. On the last day people were thrown in the water trough. At my first camp there was one pony called Tiki that was always getting out at night. At 12 at night once I went round with the instructress and we found a pony out eating the Horsehage. But it was not Tiki, it was my pony! The social side has been brilliant fun. You learn a lot at our camp about teams so you work as a group rather than as individuals. As you get older you have more responsibility at camp looking after people and helping everybody. It's really good.'

For Mark Colvin too in the Stanmore branch life has not been easy. He contends with an hereditary skin disease. As a small boy, he went to a summer camp. As he was not allowed to swim, he had extra riding lessons. His mother had ridden as a girl, so when he enjoyed it his parents arranged for him to have regular lessons. When he found that the Pony Club met regularly at the school, he joined and hired school ponies so that he could compete in tetrathlon and mounted games. Around his twelfth birthday, his parents decided to buy him a pony of his own.

Tragically, whilst Mark was abroad on a school skiing trip, his mother died in her sleep. His father says, 'This is where the Pony Club has been so good. He could have gone on the streets as boys might do, but keeping him involved in the Pony Club kept him ticking over and gradually he worked out the problems of Mum dying.' His father resolved that he must still have the pony. But fate was not kind. Within three months of its purchase 'Another horse kicked it in the field, bang, that was the end of it.' Mark and his father had a long discussion, and Mark decided that rather than buying another pony he would prefer them to move house closer to the yards: before this Mark had been bicycling some eight miles each way for every ride.

At last Mark's luck changed. A veterinary surgeon named Jackie Ross invited him to ride for her, and Mark accompanied her and her brother's family to competitions everywhere. Mark's natural feel for horses was developed and his knowledge and confidence built up. He took part in mounted games, the tetrathlon and showjumping.

Mark is now 18. He has passed his B Test and will shortly take his H Test. He is also working through his BHS exams. He is working full time in a yard. Despite a recent serious accident when he was kicked and spent 8 weeks in hospital, his enthusiasm is undiminished. He plans to earn his living by teaching, whilst dreaming of being a professional show jumper.

13

DRESSAGE

Dressage was for many years the Cinderella of the Pony Club. Small children did not see the point of 'endlessly riding round in small circles.' It remains something which has to be taught with exceptional imagination and flair to capture the interest of the average ten-year-old. The fact that most parents are equally baffled exacerbates the problem. Negotiating a series of fences seems a reasonable objective: first completing an apparently pointless ritual is incomprehensible.

A few years later the teenager notices that those friends who take trouble with their flatwork are proving more successful than the rest, not only in pure dressage tests or in the dressage phase of their eventing, but in their jumping also. The realisation that dressage is not just an end in itself but also a way of improving every facet of a horse's performance is a shock. Regret may follow for lost opportunities.

Dressage does open many doors. The likelihood of finding a pony capable of going to the top in dressage at low cost is much greater than of finding a comparable pony for any of the disciplines which involve jumping. For, provided a pony is a good mover naturally, and has a suitable temperament, its development in this field is almost entirely dependent on the skill and dedication of the rider and trainer. As soon as jumping large fences is called for, a pony with considerable natural scope is necessary, which may increase the price proportionately.

In this respect, Danny is a poor example, for he eventually proved to have scope as well. But few people would have suspected any of this at the time when the Hall family in the Holderness branch in East Yorkshire first saw him. Danny was five, and he had been pulling a cart for a farmer, but he was in disgrace for he had started to kill sheep. Seeing his livelihood at risk, the farmer tethered him by the road and was only too pleased to see him go when some friends of Mrs Hall put in an offer.

Camilla Hall was just 14. She comes from a farming family, with most of her relations interested in horses, hunting, point to pointing, schooling on horses and ponies and the Pony Club. Camilla had already moved on to a horse, but she had not really been ready to do so and was not enjoying it. She could not cope with the horse on her own and always needed supervision and help. Her mother was keen to find her 'something that she could bring on herself rather than

Graham Oakland on Wild Rose at the Dressage Championships. (Bob Langrish)

something that was very serious really; so that she could ride by herself, get off and put up a jump and get on again.'

Camilla came home from school and was taken to see the dun pony. 'I thought Oh No. I wasn't that chuffed with him when I first saw him. Then when I rode him I thought he was lovely. He moved so well and I thought he was really sweet but there were a lot of other things wrong with him. He lent on my hands and I thought he was a bit strong, but such good fun to ride and I thought he was special.' They named him, appropriately, Can Be Done, known as Danny.

Camilla was always quite keen on dressage. 'It's pretty interesting: when you do things right it does all happen. Especially with Danny, he does help, he tries for you. You have to be very good at dressage to event. If you can do dressage you can really do it all; it helps your showjumping and everything.' When she first had him, Camilla took him in Working Hunter Pony classes, and qualified him for Peterborough; hunted him ('he was the best hunter ever, he would jump anything, a huge Holderness ditch and he just crept down and leaped'); took her B Test on him; and when school friends came to stay they all rode him. 'He couldn't have got where he did without his paces, but his temperament was really helpful. He was quite strong but he thought about me and he was quite human. He would try and do what I asked him. He was also incredibly cheeky and very confident in himself. He wanted to be boss of the others. He thought he was the most special thing in the yard, which he was, and he never knew he was too small to be boss. That made you love him more. We had a special little relationship.'

Camilla was also having weekly dressage lessons with Mrs Oakland, the Pony Club Area Representative. As everyone began to appreciate his potential he was kept more and more for dressage only. Not only did Danny qualify for Weston Park for the Dressage Championships in two successive years, the first year as part of the Holderness team and the second year having won the Area Dressage competition, but he only just missed being longlisted for the British International team trials. Camilla blames herself: 'I made some mistakes. I clicked at him and marks were taken off for using my voice.' Plans for trying again the following year had to be given up when the age groups were changed, and eventually the family reluctantly decided to sell Danny, as Camilla was outgrowing him.

The Hall family have always sold their horses and ponies, but Danny was special. Mrs Hall remembers people coming to see him and 'they didn't like this and they didn't like that. I kept thinking 'if you say one thing you don't like you're not having him. ' It wasn't really the point.' Eventually the ideal home was found for Danny in Kent where he is fully appreciated. Even so, Camilla says, 'I'm not sentimental about horses, but when Danny went it was the first and last time I've ever cried about a pony.' He had taught Camilla so much and learnt so much himself: he could even be turned out in a field with sheep before he left.

Young competitor at Fernie Hunt Branch Dressage and Show Jumping, 1992. *(A. & B. Sorohan: Event Prints)*

(above) Dressage: Camilla Hall and
Can Be Done at Weston Park 1992
(see page 78)
(Pleasure Prints, Crookham Common)

PLATE SEVEN

(left) Tetrathlon: Rose Buxton and
Mr Jake having just completed the
riding phase at the
1993 Championships (see page 99)
(James Buxton)

(left) Polocrosse: a young player
(Iain Burns)

PLATE EIGHT

(below) Polo: a Handley Cross match in 1988: Charlotte Hastings centre front (see page 115)
(Max Hastings)

— 14 —

HUNTING

As the Christmas holidays approach, many members count the days not only to Christmas but also to the Pony Club Meet or Children's Meet. Most hunts allocate a special day when adults are only allowed to come out hunting if they are accompanying a child or otherwise helping. Children, or in some cases Pony Club members only, pay a specially reduced sum. At the meet, the Master usually gives a little talk, reminding the children of points to be careful about during the day: making sure that they do not let their pony kick another pony or a hound, shutting all gates, avoiding damage by keeping close into the side of the field if they go round a drilled field, the debt they all owe to the farmers, and avoiding holding up traffic on the roads. Then older members are usually selected and given the chance to accompany the huntsman and the whipper-in. After an hour or so, the first members will probably come back to join the rest of the field, or mounted followers, and another member will be given the opportunity to join one or other of the hunt staff, and thus see exactly what really happens during a day's hunting.

Historically, the Pony Club has close links with hunting, for the original branches were all started in, and named after, the different hunts. Today, there is no pressure whatever on any member to go hunting. There is merely the opportunity in most branches for members to find out for themselves about hunting, through coming out at a cheap rate on the specially allocated days or taking part in such activities as visits to the kennels. There is no formal link financially between Pony Club branches and the hunt: certainly the hunt does not benefit from the Pony Club, but sometimes the Pony Club may benefit from the hunt, by using hunt property, be it Hunt Supporters' showjumps, or premises for camps or rallies. Many hunting people too, with no other connection with the Pony Club, offer facilities for members' use: a swimming pool during camp, perhaps, or hunt jumps round their farm for a cross-country course.

For many Pony Club members, hunting is not limited to once or twice a year at the Children's or Pony Club meet, but a sport to be enjoyed regularly throughout the season, and not just by those whose parents are involved. Thomas Berry in the Fitzwilliam can sometimes go with his brother Richard, who enjoys hunting although he is less keen than Thomas on other aspects of riding, but neither of their parents hunt. Thomas not only loves the excitement of riding across-country, but is also keen to learn as much as he can about the sport. In the Fitzwilliam country, members are expected to take a hunting test before coming out unaccompanied (in other hunting countries, passing the Pony Club C Test is all that is required). Thomas found working for this an interesting exercise. Unlike some children and adults, he certainly does not hunt for social reasons: although his two closest friends, Oliver and Philip, both enjoy hunting as much as he does, they are rarely out together, for Oliver is away at school so can only hunt in the holidays whereas Philip has to go to school on Saturday mornings, and so often does not appear until Thomas's pony is ready to be taken home.

Joanne Syckelmoore hunts with the Garth and South Berks, where anti-hunting demonstrators are often active. After helping somebody by holding a horse for them, she recently found herself alone in a field when the demonstrators closed the gate to prevent her leaving and hurled foul-mouthed abuse at her and the elderly lady who owned the field. When Joanne eventually managed to go through the gate, a car was driven so that it almost touched her pony's hocks, briefly trapping the pony between two cars.

Members should not be sent out hunting unaccompanied (except at the Children's Meet) until they have passed their C Test, and even then there should always be a reliable older person in contact at least from a car and preferably mounted. Younger and less experienced riders do often need help. Other hunting people will naturally help if they can, but they cannot be expected, for example, to give up their day to escorting a child round by the gates if they come to a fence which is too big for pony or rider.

Jane Kerswell has young rider Rebecca Bosworth out on a leading rein. *(Jim Meads)*

Pony Club Riders being briefed by the Field Master at a Children's Meet. *(Jim Meads)*

Every member should have the opportunity to see for themselves what happens on a day's hunting so that they can make up their own minds on this controversial issue. Mrs Dixey, DC of the Whaddon Chase branch, remembers escorting four members who had not been hunting before. 'They couldn't believe how often the hunted fox actually got away. Children need to understand that foxes can be killed instantly by hounds or you can allow gassing or snaring or shooting and that's a wicked way for any animal to die. You don't do your children any favours if you try to protect them from what happens in the real world.'

Natalie Bucklar of the Axe Vale branch in Devon remembers how 'we took the Axe Vale hounds out exercising once, round the lanes and through a few fields, then we came back and had a video and a quiz on hunting. It was really good. We learnt quite a lot.' She started hunting with her first pony. 'I always knew about the Boxing Day Hunt and just wanted to go. From then on I just really enjoyed it and went.'

Unlike Natalie, the two Vallance brothers in the Bicester country belong to a hunting family. They feel that hunting regularly has helped them enormously with riding across-country, giving them the confidence to ride on into their fences and giving them stronger, more balanced seats. Through hunting they can establish more confidence between horse and rider and young, green ponies become enthusiastic about jumping fences. The Bicester branch also has a mock hunt, at the end of the summer holidays, with the huntsman in his scarlet coat blowing the horn, members dressed up as hounds and an older member as the fox. The Master or huntsman sometimes also gives a talk, explaining how he communicates with his hounds.

Many members, Marcus Vallance thinks, would like to come hunting but are afraid that their pony will be too strong. If some of the instructors come out at the Children's Meet, they can help here because they know the individuals and their ponies and can often suggest solutions: many ponies are less difficult than their riders anticipate, or a change of bit may make all the difference.

Another Bicester member, Jo Eeley, who is 14, also loves hunting. 'If it's near here I can go. If my pony is fit enough to stay out, I like it when it gets to about two o'clock and people tend to go away and you have a good run then and jump everything. Or if you have a good run and people who aren't jumping go to the back, and you start off at the back because you think "my pony will get too excited if I go to the front" and then most of the time she jumps everything and you just end up at the front.' Her mother remembers on one occasion, when she herself was queueing for a hunt jump, she suddenly saw Jo sailing over some enormous Gas Board rails behind one of the more dashing members of the hunt. She was not reassured to see Jo's pilot shortly afterwards taking on a 5 ft 6 in. stone wall on to tarmac, and realised that he was obviously in no fit state to be taking such decisions, having had too much to drink. But Jo was using her brains, and was wisely no longer following him. Hunting does help members to learn to think for themselves and ponies tend to go much better with hounds than they do alone in a competitive environment.

South Shropshire Pony Club member Suzanne Warner riding up with huntsman Michael Rowson. *(Jim Meads)*

15

EUROPE AND BEYOND

The Pony Club has kept pace with the trend towards Europe, and joint enterprises, official and unofficial, are common. The most formal links come through the Euro Pony Club, an organisation which arranges exchanges between individuals and also Eurocamps for children from a range of European nations. The first of these camps was held in England, the second in Germany and the third in France. There are plans to hold more than one a year in future. Anyone interested should contact Mrs Angela Yeoman of Southfield House, Whatley, Near Frome, Somerset BA11 3JY, Telephone number 0373 836209.

Tracy Aughton, of the Thetford Chase branch in Norfolk, was one of four English members to attend the Eurocamp in Germany. She heard about it through an advertisment in *Horse and Hound*. At 17 she was the oldest of the four, and the only boy, Tom, was the youngest at 14. Although the group was not restricted to those taking German at school, as Tracey at first understood it would be, 'We all spoke enough German. I think Tom struggled a bit but he managed to get by with sign language.' The British contingent made contact beforehand though eventually they all travelled out independently.

There were four teenagers each from England, Austria, France, Holland and Berlin. The Germans brought their own ponies, and the others were mounted there. The horses were 'all very well schooled but they hadn't done anything like hacking out. They were fed on nothing but oats and hay. I don't suppose they were used to any other type of lifestyle so it wasn't so bad.' The instruction was at C+ to B level, and once the English group had 'worked out what walk trot and canter were the rest was quite easy.' The French, on the other hand, 'never quite got to grips with the language.'

Tracy found the teaching more technical than at home, with great emphasis on 'really getting the horse to go.' Most of the time was spent on flat work: 'Mind you, it was probably safer. The horse I had to jump, every time you faced it at a fence it sort of cleared off.'

They were taken to watch a One-Day Event, which did not resemble a British one. All four team members did their dressage in the same arena together, and when they had later to show their horses in hand the impression was very Germanic, as they turned their heads rigidly in military style.

The atmosphere in camp was extremely friendly with 'sixteen girls all crammed into one tent and the four boys had a really nice tent all to themselves.'

Eurocamp.
(Iain Burns)

They were told that 'we were going to do some stable management type things but we never did. We never cleaned tack either. When we offered to clean tack at the end of the week they looked at us as if to say 'What do you want to do that for?' They all thought we were really strange when we did clean it before we went home.' Safety standards too were very different from those in the British Pony Club. During a chaotic canter on the first day, 'only two of us got kicked. One girl was on crutches for the rest of the week. I just hobbled about with a lovely lump on my leg.'

Tracy considers it was 'definitely an experience worth going for. Ridingwise it gave me some fresh ideas: never a bad thing really. You come back and use them on your own horse.'

Many children today become involved in French exchanges. Frequently the experience is disappointing, with those involved having few shared interests, so that they are bored, or actually miserable, and gain little from the opportunity. This was not the case for twelve members of the Grafton Pony Club.

It began when the DC of the Grafton, Mrs Wyman, had a telephone call from Pony Club Headquarters. They had been contacted by a French organisation with no connection whatsoever with the British Pony Club, except that it called itself the 'Poney Club d'Hardelot', and some members wished to do an exchange with members of an English branch. The Grafton was chosen as it was a country branch but reasonably accessible to London. Unfortunately this was in the middle of camp week, too late for much to be organised that summer, but a notice on the camp notice board led to a few members volunteering to have French visitors that summer. Shortly afterwards, six French children came to stay with three different English families. The whole group went to the Pony Club Championships at Weston Park. A Fun Day already organised for under twelves was amended to include the 12 and 13-year-old visitors on borrowed ponies, and a bilingual element introduced. The ice was broken and preparations began in earnest for the following year.

The English organisers remember mainly the details which they now feel they could have improved for their European visitors. A misunderstanding resulted in the French children arriving at six in the morning rather than six in the evening when they attended the Grafton camp next summer, and producing suitable ponies was not easy. But for the visitors themselves everything was new and exciting. After riding round a cross-country course, 14-year-old Charlotte declared that she would like to come back to the same place 'tomorrow and the next day, *faire le gallop.*' Whilst Grafton campers do not actually sleep in tents, one family delighted their guests by arranging a stay under canvas, which was something the French children had never previously tried.

Then it was the turn of the Grafton members, and the ten girls and two boys were crammed into two vehicles driven by parents to board the ferry. This was one of several measures which enabled the cost of the enterprise to be kept at a level which meant that, whilst the full expense was borne by the families involved and not by the Pony Club, no member was likely to be left out because of the price. After a somewhat stormy crossing, they were warmly welcomed by the French families and driven to Hardelot, which is conveniently close to Boulogne. Their hosts had laid on a picnic lunch and a conducted tour of the premises for the whole of the English party, parents included. Long before their parents departed, the English children were feeling that they had found a home from home.

The 'Poney Club d'Hardelot' bore little resemblance to its British near-namesake, being more a mixture of riding school and country club. Some eighty horses and ponies were crammed in every corner, six Shetlands sharing a single small stable, which was held together by pieces of string. Most of the riders were children whose parents had weekend cottages close by, apparently selected partly because of the Poney Club, which was such an important part of local life that the pavements were specially sanded and horses had priority on them, although speed was officially frowned on. The British group, used to the high standards of stable management taught by their own Pony Club with ponies receiving individual attention in private homes, later wrote of their reactions, starting when they watched 'a Beginners' lesson where six four-year-olds were put on Shetlands and chased around the indoor school at a gallop with a lunge whip until one fell off! We thought that this was an interesting way to teach people to ride but at least it taught them to have a good seat! As for their clothes, we didn't think that a flimsy bit of plastic without a strap that didn't fit for a hat, and shorts and trainers, were really adequate to ride in! The horses were not much better equipped as some of their bridles only consisted of an headpiece, a bit and reins that didn't match or do up at the buckle! Also, the saddles with surcingles over the top instead of girths were interesting. However these were mere details and we soon began to enjoy ourselves, especially when we found out that having a pony in France does not include having to muck out, feed, water or clean the horses or the tack! We thought that this was a brilliant idea and gave us more time for other things.'

Riding lessons in French were an interesting challenge for the visitors. 'I was in front and being told to change the rein was a bit confusing', remarked one Grafton member, to which her mother uncharitably commented 'But you get confused in England!' Certainly taking part in so many activities as well as living in French families meant that all the children improved remarkably in their French.

Travelling conditions did shock the English group: 'When they went to the event they had a big lorry and trailer and they really did crush them in like sardines. There were no partitions and they were all on different levels so when the brakes were slammed on they all fell over.' Standards of turn-out too did not match those of the British Pony Club. In Britain, the Grafton members had been quite impressed: 'All the children when they came to England had navy blue jackets and little gold buttons and things, and they looked really smart, but they didn't take as much care about the horses tackwise'. This, however, applied only to equipment belonging to the Club and not to the privately owned tack.

But when it came to riding, French standards were quite as high as English ones. There was a series of tests which the French children were expected to take, and each one's level of achievement was recorded, together with insurance and medical details, in the record book carried by each French boy or girl. A number of them were taking part in showjumping or dressage at a relatively advanced level, competing on equal terms with adults. One French boy in particular, Julien, who exchanged with Chris Gardner, much impressed the Grafton members with his high standard of horsemanship. Unlike his compatriots, he had a pony of his own which was not ridden by anyone else at the Poney Club. But English honour was upheld: as they wrote later, 'On our last day in Hardelot our hosts arranged a showjumping competition in which, although we were rather intimidated by the size of the fences and the fact that we were all riding unknown horses, we did altogether better than the French

The Grafton visit to France: *(back row l to r)* Susanna Waters, Georgina Rolt, Camilla Hodges, Melissa Gibb, Mme. Rohmer, Sally Willoughby, Shelley Wisner; *(seated l to r)* Ruth Haynes, Catherine Rolt, Amy Willoughby, Chris Gardner, Charles Henson, Katie Hodges. *(Christopher Gardner)*

and came back with a fourth, a fifth and a cup for the best English rider who had been riding a horse that had been eliminated twice with the French!'

Perhaps the key to the success of the whole enterprise was the way in which the common interest in riding created a deeper bond between all concerned. The French families were quite exceptionally hospitable, generous and welcoming. Soon children of both nationalities were sharing the excitements of Mini Golf, Fun Parks, swimming in the Channel and 'causing chaos in a Creperie' as well as galloping on the beach and in the forest. Many have struck up lasting friendships, and neither constant rain during their time in France nor a Force 10 gale during the crossing home have done anything to dampen their desire for future exchanges. All the twelve Grafton members were still, many months later, bubbling over with enthusiasm as they recalled exciting rides, adventures shared, new experiences and, above all, warm, friendly people.

The Axe Vale branch in Devon has regular expeditions to Europe. 'We've just literally taken off in the mini bus, packed loads of food in, taken one gas stove for everyone and travelled through France,' says Chrissy Howick. 'Mrs Sleight (the

DC) will pick certain places and ring up youth hostels and book us in and then we'll just try and make it in time and stop on the sides of the roads and get all the camping gear out and things like that. She's very forceful, she won't be afraid to write to people and keep hammering them. The way we got tickets for the Spanish Riding School at Vienna, I think they initially wrote back and said "No it was impossible". Mrs Sleight kept writing back saying they should do more for younger people and in the end we got tickets. They've been very good, those trips. She takes about three adults.'

In Vienna, the performance at the Spanish Riding School more than lived up to the highest expectations. Members also enjoyed their visit to 'the famous Cafe Sacher, and amongst the fur coats, silk dresses and dinner jackets we were not that conspicuous– worn out, wearing rugby shirts, jeans and trainers!!...'

After six such earlier excursions, Barcelona for the Olympics when they had a former member (Mary Thomson) in the team was an obvious choice. Despite the inevitable disappointments, in Mrs Sleight's words, 'We had done it, we were there, we supported Mary through triumph and disaster.'

With a train to catch, as soon as the medals had been presented, there was a mad rush for the Metro. Natalie Bucklar and her friend were holding an end each of their British flag. In their haste, they unintentionally 'wrapped this poor foreign girl up and Mrs Sleight thought it was one of us mucking around so she hit her over the head and said "Will you get a move on girl!".' The poor foreign girl emerged from the flag to an apologetic Mrs Sleight and a group of members who just managed to climb on the train before collapsing with laughter.

When Peter Brackett first joined the Isle of Man branch in the early 1980s, activities were restricted to a few instructional rallies and an annual camp. All that soon changed when a link was formed with the Haydock Park branch, who initially invited a team of Manx members, including Peter, to take part in the Area competition of the Prince Philip Cup on ponies lent by the Haydock Park members. So successful was the visit, in every way, that the Island branch was soon raising the money to send over teams with their own ponies for the Cup, and later for the Area tetrathlon and Horse Trials as well. Close links were formed with other mainland branches, including Saddleworth and Pendle Forest and Craven, with members of these branches crossing the Irish Sea for 'fun weekends'.

Peter had not originally been a very keen rider, but was cajoled into taking part to take over his sister's outgrown pony. But 'the fun of the mounted games, exhileration and competitiveness of the tetrathlon and the rapport amongst the branches' motivated him into learning more, and this in turn eventually took him across the world. Success in the 'B' Test led to the offer of a job in Switzerland, looking after horses for a family in Fribourg who gave him a wonderful time and still remain friends.

Two years later, in 1988, 'the Pony Club, in conjunction with the *Daily Mail*

Axe Vale Members loading up for Barcelona and the Olympics and *(below)* with their banner in Barcelona. *(Mrs Sleight)*

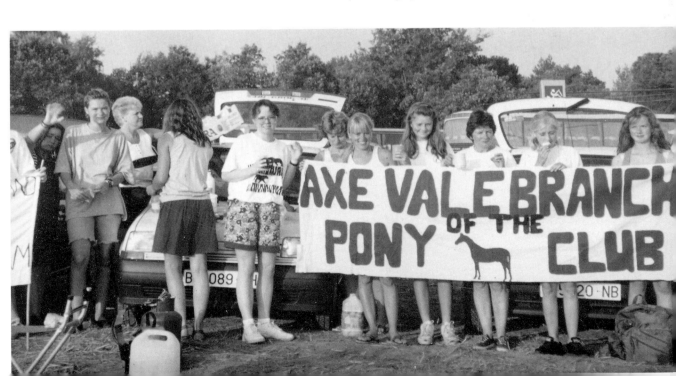

and QANTAS, ran a competition to send eight people from Britain to Australia as part of the country's bicentennial celebrations. I applied and was amazed when I received notification that I was chosen to attend a selection weekend, to be held at Stoneleigh. The selection process was over the two days, in which the thirty successful applicants were examined in riding and stable management, and were interviewed by a panel. At the end of the weekend, which by itself was great fun, the organisers confronted the thirty of us and told us that instead of informing us by letter, which we were expecting, they were going to tell us there and then! I don't think the realisation of being chosen actually dawned on me until I was boarding the plane at Heathrow.

'I travelled to Darwin with a fellow winner, but upon arrival at Darwin we were split up and stayed with families. After a few days in Darwin, we were flown down to Alice Springs where we met with the rest of the group, who had come from all over Australia – more friends to meet! The next day we loaded our 'swags' on board a coach and set off on what I think was probably the longest and most uncomfortable journey of my life, towards our destined cattle ranches. I shall never forget the feeling of total bewilderment when we arrived at 'home' for the next few weeks. Basically, a stunted tree marked the place where we were to set camp. No tent, no toilets, showers, etc.; just dust!

'The time at the cattle station was the most exciting experience of my life. We carried out all sorts of jobs with the rest of the "ringers", including droving the cattle from the outlying areas into the station and working on the cattle within the station. It really was like something out of a western-type movie! After we had worked on the station, we joined the other group from another station and headed back towards Darwin by coach, seeing the sights as we went.' (See picture on page 105.)

Peter feels very strongly that his 'personal achievements were made possible by the dedication and enthusiasm of, primarily, the Isle of Man branch of the Pony Club and, later, the Pony Club in general. The Isle of Man branch opened up many opportunities for me and, for this, I am very grateful.'

16

TETRATHLON

For the all round sportsman who enjoys riding across-country, there is nothing to compare with the tetrathlon. An adaptation of the Olympic sport of Modern Pentathlon, competitors have to swim, shoot and run as well as ride. Separate classes are held for the different age groups, with Open classes, Junior classes for those under fifteen and Minimus classes for younger members. Boys and girls do not compete against each other, and older boys run further and swim for longer than do girls.

In the running phase each competitor is timed over a measured cross-country route. The Senior Boys cover a distance of 3,000 metres, for the Senior Girls and Juniors the distance is half this, and the Minimus competitors have only 1,000 metres to run. For the swimming phase, a fixed time is allowed of 4, 3 or 2 minutes, and the score worked out according to the distance covered in the time. Shooting is with an air pistol at a target 10 metres away in Open classes and 7 metres for younger competitors. In the Minimus, competitors are allowed to hold the gun in both hands. The riding is round a cross-country course, of a size appropriate to the competitors' age, which will include both a gate to be opened and shut, and a slip rail where the rider has to dismount, move a slip rail, lead his pony over a second rail a few inches above the ground, put back the slip rail and climb back on the pony in less than sixty seconds.

It all sounds somewhat daunting. Yet in practice there is nothing which is beyond the ability of the average healthy seven-year-old rider, provided he or she can swim. Pistol shooting is something new to almost everybody, and, whilst those who go on to take the sport seriously will eventually want a gun of their own, beginners will use a Club gun, and only under close supervision. There will always be somebody responsible in charge whenever the guns are being used, safety rules are strictly enforced and all members are taught to be safety conscious long before they learn to shoot more accurately.

You may feel that you could never excel at four such different sports. Few of even the most successful competitors do. Natalie Gerard of the Fernie, who has qualified for the Championships most years since she was 12 and at 15 was in the England team, says: 'I must admit I find the running quite hard. I still have to work very hard at it. I only enjoy it once it's over I must admit!'

The tetrathlon was originally restricted to boys and the Area competitions were not opened to girls until 1981 when Natalie was eight. When her older

Fernie Girls Tetrathlon team which won the Championships in 1987: *(l to r)* Ninga Polito, Natalie Gerard, Wanda Gerard and Helen Titterington. *(Carolyn Gerard)*

sister Wanda went along to watch a boys' tetrathlon, their parents immediately recognised that here was something which the whole family could enjoy. At first there were no separate classes for juniors or 'minis', but this did not deter Wanda or Natalie. perhaps because both embody the sporting outlook that they are taking part for pleasure and not with a view to winning. Natalie takes this refreshingly unfashionable approach for granted. 'Well, otherwise I think you wouldn't enjoy it – it loses the fun,' she says, adding that the majority of those with an over-competitive outlook, either their own or imposed on them by their parents, eventually find the pressures too great and give up completely. Certainly the welcoming smiles and uncritical encouragement offered by the Gerard girls to younger members have helped others and fostered a continuing enthusiasm for and indeed success in tetrathlon in the branch.

Wanda and Natalie owe much of their success to the support they have received from their parents. Not only have the needs of the children and their ponies always been given priority, but Mr and Mrs Gerard both worked remarkably hard to build up the branch tetrathlon teams. Their efforts were first rewarded when Natalie was twelve ('and very nervous!' she says) and the team came second to the Cottesmore in the Area competition, thus qualifying for the Championships. 'I was absolutely over the moon,' Natalie recalls. 'I was surprised I could even shoot the gun I was so excited.' Having only been second in their Area however, hopes were not running high. So, when the Cottesmore won the Championships and they themselves came fourth, their delight knew no bounds. After that Natalie never looked back. Two years later, the Fernie girls won the Championships, and Natalie's many successes have included some gained, both individually and as a team member, when representing her region and, before a change in the system, her country. She has made many excellent friends all over Britain. She does work hard at it, but, because 'I enjoy anything that involves a bit of sport', work and pleasure are, sometimes, hard to distinguish: 'I find the shooting very interesting. In the summer I practice every day. I enjoy swimming. Running – well!'

Having the right pony is particularly important in the early days. Natalie had a much loved small pony when she started, then later graduated to the 14.2 Cairo. He was originally bought for Wanda, who did not at first appreciate the strongly made chestnut, having dreamed of a thoroughbred. At that time, too, 'he hadn't done an awful lot; he got round, but stopped and jumped at every fence.' But Wanda worked hard with him, achieving more than even her family appreciated. The first time that Natalie took him to a tetrathlon all went well until they reached the gate. 'I just trotted up to it, leant forward to undo the catch and off he went' – jumping the gate. Wanda then mentioned that when she rode round the bridle paths on her own, she never opened any gates, but jumped them all.

Despite Cairo's brilliance across-country, regular competitions at senior level over the big courses set for tetrathlons are asking a lot of any animal. Natalie therefore gradually did less of the other Pony Club activities, no longer asking Cairo to compete in showjumping competitions, or the Area Horse Trials team. They continued to enjoy camp for a little longer, and regularly took part in rallies. As he has become older, he has not always been sound enough for all the tetrathlons, and Natalie is extremely grateful to kind friends who have lent her horses or ponies on these occasions. Indeed, there was a summer when Cairo needed a complete break and Natalie decided to give up the sport altogether. However, finding to her surprise that she was suffering from severe withdrawal symptoms, she soon reconsidered.

For her last summer in the Pony Club, in 1993, she found a replacement for Cairo, who is enjoying a well earned retirement. Her new horse, Little Man, gave her clear rounds at both the Area and the Championships. At the Area she attained the remarkable score of 1,000 points for shooting, or ten bull's eyes with ten shots. Had she done the same at the Championships, she would have been placed even higher than her 4th position individually. Now, sadly, Little Man has been sold, for she will have less time for riding and in Modern Pentathlon horses are provided. Natalie is busy practising her fencing.

The Individual winner in the 1993 Girls' Championship was Kate Allenby, from the Spooners and West Dartmoor branch. Like Natalie, she is fully conscious of all she owes to the Pony Club. 'When I first joined I couldn't ride for toffee. If my friends had said when I was ten that I would ride in America and

Ireland I wouldn't have believed it. I've learnt an awful lot: I was atrocious when I started. Most of my friends I've met through the Pony Club: I've got an awful lot out of it. It's supported me in whatever I've wanted to do.'

But Kate did not always see the Pony Club in such a positive light. She remembers when she joined at 11 going to her first Working Rally: 'One of the most boring things I ever went to but I met a couple of people and someone to ride with, so it immediately became more fun.' At the time, with her limited knowledge of horsemanship, she saw no point in 'trotting round in circles' and still has reservations about teaching which is not sufficiently imaginative for younger children. 'I actually prefer stable management rallies to ordinary ones; I've realised the importance of it.' She felt that the regime was much stricter then than it is now and considered the instructors 'awfully picky over the dress code', though through this she first learnt 'the necessity to get organised and to be tidy in the horsey world'. One particular instructor remains in her mind from an early camp: immaculately turned out in long hunting boots and a bowler, he soon irritated Kate by insisting that she ride in a snaffle not a Kimblewick, with the result that she seemed constantly to be 'tanking back towards the lines.' Instructors and members alike rode their horses and ponies to the river for water. The instructor's horse made camp for Kate by suddenly rolling. The instructor sank: even his bowler hat was beneath the water.

Tests too are an aspect of Pony Club which does not impress Kate. She sees test results as erratic because of the difficulty of maintaining the same standard. 'I'd had tests up to my ears by the time I'd finished C+'.

All the same, Kate cannot 'think of any organisation that does so well at teaching children, as well as being good mannered and tidy, to have so much fun. Camp is one of the best things: it was brilliant.' Better still, there are all the competitions. Kate has represented her branch at Area level in the Prince Philip Cup (which she thinks 'just brilliant for juniors; it gets the rider to think about other things as well as riding'), horse trials and showjumping, though tetrathlon remains her first love. She finds it a very sociable sport, a point made by several tetrathletes, because of the long breaks between the phases without the necessity to devote every spare moment to the horse. Despite her success, like Natalie, she is much appreciated in her branch for the support she gives to the younger members.

The visit to Canada and the United States in 1992 was a tremendous opportunity for the five boys and five girls who went. Kate loved the chance to see so much of the world and to make friends from different continents. James Whetman of the Four Burrow in Cornwall also enjoyed the sightseeing, but was somewhat more cynical about the other teams and, in particular, the horses which he and his team mates were offered to ride: the excitement on the riding front for him was returning to England two days before the Championships and getting on his own horse after five weeks.

The horse problem did not arise for Julia Allen of the Old Berkshire. In Canada, 'I went into this girl's house and there was a picture of my horse on top of her television. I couldn't believe it. I didn't recognise the girl but she'd borrowed my horse at Lincoln when they'd come over (to Britain) so they made special arrangements for me to borrow her horse when I was in Canada. He was a super eventer: I think I was the envy of all because he was a lovely, lovely horse. I think some of the boys' horses were a bit rough but I had three horses that gave me three clear rounds so I couldn't complain at all.'

Julia found the journey out somewhat amusing as the British contingent prepared to board the aeroplane complete with their own guns and huge boxes of tea, not for their own consumption but for their hosts as the expedition was sponsored by Typhoo. Soon she was enjoying the excitements of white water rafting, but did on occasion find the heat oppressive. For one run in Canada the temperature was so high that competitors were at first told that they could dispense with number cloths, merely writing their numbers on their legs instead, though this was later reversed lest they should be so hot and sweaty that the numbers would run. In the photograph, even Julia's constant delightful smile has vanished in the heat, although the running is the phase at which she excels. One highlight for her was a visit to a family where the father was a vet who had trained at Cambridge in England and started the pentathlon there. Julia accompanied him on his rounds for a day, for she herself is a veterinary student at Cambridge. With her customary modesty she attributes even this success, despite the three grade 'A' A Levels required to obtain a place, to the Pony Club: 'Doing tetrathlon meant that I wanted to go to Cambridge to do the pentathlon, so I probably wouldn't have got to Cambridge without the Pony Club.'

Julia did not join the Pony Club until she was 11 and before that 'I didn't really have the instruction. We never had transport. For my first ride we had to go round at sitting trot then we had to shout out our ages and

Julia Allen completing the Running phase in Canada.

The Shooting Phase at Area 6 Tetrathlon 1993. *(James Buxton)*

I was in the bottom ride with five- and six-year-olds but I soon progressed to my own age group. We had this nasty pony and I had ridden it but not very keenly. Then we got this one that I could just mooch around on and kick; it was very dozey but at least I felt confident to go out and ride. I was eliminated usually at the first fence for three refusals but I suppose it taught me to use my legs.'

Julia soon took to Pony Club with her customary enthusiasm. 'I think it is the most fantastic thing that ever existed really. I still do all the rallies. I can't believe I will be too old. I don't know what I'll do without it. Camp was really brilliant. We used to count down the days from about 364 I think!' In a recent discussion on the family caravan, her father remarked that you could not have six people in it. Julia, recollecting camp, replied 'One night, Daddy, we had nineteen in there!'

Even though her riding at first was limited, she was already a keen swimmer. 'I'd read about tetrathlon but we didn't have it in our branch so I told my Mum that I wanted to do it and she rang up another lady and she said 'there's no manager' but suggested they should be joint managers and start it off.'

Like most tetrathletes, Julia has one Achilles heel. 'My shooting is diabolical. I got 680 (out of a possible 1,000) at my Area. I got 760 in one recent competition and I think I was about the happiest person around. My swim, run and ride go all right' (an understatement since Julia won the Individual Championship in 1992 and was second in it in 1993) 'but the coach says "don't worry if you're shaking, you'll still hit the ten" but I don't think he realises I'm shaking either side of the target.' In America there was once a problem when the electronic mechanism for turning the targets did not work correctly. Competitors were asked whether they wished to reshoot, on condition that if they did so they must accept the second set of scores. Julia thought that she could not possibly do any worse, 'but I did, so I had to accept a worse score, which probably served me right.'

Tetrathlon in the Pony Club succeeds in combining a marvellously friendly atmosphere with an extremely high standard of competition. At the 1993 Championships, nobody was cheering Kate Allenby in from her run harder than Julia Allen, well aware though she was that those few vital seconds were destroying her own chances of a second victory. Yet outsiders are often unaware of the standard attained by the top competitors: perhaps the name 'Pony Club' conveys an image of children at play, not young athletes competing against the best of their contemporaries. 'The Championships are so amazing and the standard's so high.'

Yet, because it is a team competition as well as an individual one, participation in the Championships is within the reach of the ordinary member with no particular skills at running, shooting or swimming. Rose Buxton is a member of the Fernie Hunt branch, as is Natalie Gerard. Natalie and another keen tetrathlete, Gillian Robinson, looking round for eligible members with a reasonable chance of going clear across-country if nothing else, asked Rose and another member to help them make up a girls' team for the Area competition. Rose has taken part in occasional tetrathlons all her life, but says that 'the target has often not had any holes in it after I've shot at it, and for the running phase I generally walked as soon as I was out of sight!' Nor is she a particularly fast swimmer. However she made an effort to train hard in the fortnight leading up to the Area competition, and the 15 hand skewbald cob Mr Jake which she recently took over from her brother jumped a clear round. With Natalie's outstanding score and Gillian's excellent one, the team qualified for the Championships, although the fourth member of the team had to be changed because of holiday commitments. Rose will long remember the three days she spent at Moreton Morrell, where the Championships are held. Although she did not enjoy the run, she did not disgrace herself in her total score, had a superb ride round the cross-country course to score the maximum 1400 points, and shared in the very special atmosphere and team spirit which is such a feature of the Tetrathlon Championships.

The tetrathlon was originally started to encourage boys to continue riding, and was restricted to them. Although today more girls than boys compete, the tetrathlon remains popular with boys, many of whom are excellent riders across-country but lack the patience, or perhaps merely the interest, required for dressage. Other boys are all-round athletes whose interest in the horse is kept alight by their enthusiasm for the sport as a whole. A third category includes those boys who, like so many of the girls, are excellent horsemen and are competing with equal enthusiasm in horse trials, showjumping and possibly dressage as well.

James Whetman of the Four Burrow is adamant that he 'Definitely would not have started riding if it wasn't for the Tet. I joined at six or seven to do the Tet. My sister did lots of eventing and stuff, but I've never been to camp, except on the first day once because Mum was helping.' His friends agree that 'James did not join to go to rallies, that's for sure', but also point out that he has competed regularly and successfully in horse trials as well as tetrathlons. Like many others, girls and boys alike, the primary object of membership for him is to be able to compete. To do so at the highest level is inevitably a major commitment. Not only must he train in all four disciplines on a regular basis, but ensure also that he is supremely fit. He achieves this by belonging to a swimming club as well as the Pony Club and spending spare time on such work as hay baling.

Prize Giving at Area 6 Tetrathlon 1993. *(Hugh Buxton)*

Clare Fraser from the same branch has qualified for the Championships on numerous occasions, often as an individual, despite declaring herself 'allergic to running'. Once, when the Championships were immediately after an International competition for which she was also selected, her performance in every phase was 'my worst everything, basically.' Such occasions are inevitably particularly exhausting for competitors and horses coming from remote parts of Britain. The Four Burrow now tend to travel up two days before the Championships start. Despite the challenges, Cornwall has been outstandingly successful at tetrathlon: Charlie Low, Boy's Individual Champion in 1991, 1992 and 1993, comes from the East Cornwall branch.

For Michael and Tim Ferens in the Bicester country in Oxfordshire, the tetrathlon has certainly been the reason they have kept up their interest in horses. Their father, a veterinary surgeon, is the tetrathlon organiser for the branch. In his opinion 'boys lose interest with messing about with horses. They like to jump on the back of a horse thinking it's like a motor car.' He is remarkably successful at making tetrathlon fun for boys with this approach whilst helping them to develop their riding ability as well. Whilst Michael eventually gave up riding aged 17 because he found that 'the senior running got on top of me', he was soon back in the saddle a year later when working in New Zealand, and Tim at 17 continues to ride whilst planning to follow his father into the veterinary profession.

Both Malcolm Clapson, the moving spirit behind so much in the Staff College and Sandhurst branch, and Marty Fields, enjoying all the Spooners and West Dartmoor branch has to offer despite the shortage of other boys, would probably rate the tetrathlon as their favourite activity of all in the Pony Club. Marty had the inspiring example of Kate Allenby to follow and Malcolm belonged to the winning team in the Championship in 1989. It is undoubtedly a sport with tremendous appeal for the enthusiastic all rounder, boy or girl, whether single mindedly devoted to it or enjoying it as an extension of everything else the Pony Club has to offer.

17

THE PONY CLUB
OVERSEAS

The Pony Club is a world wide organisation with nearly 2,000 branches in seventeen different countries outside the United Kingdom. Clubs in other countries are self governing but are affiliated to the Pony Club of Great Britain provided that their individual rules 'incorporate the objects and spirit of the rules of the Pony Club'. The two countries with the greatest number of branches are Australia, with 927, and the USA with 510, compared with 366 in the United Kingdom. These are followed by Canada and New Zealand, with 162 and 82 respectively. Whilst Eire comes after these, with just 56 branches, its geographical proximity leads to close contacts and frequent exchange visits, and also means that Irish teams are able to compete in the United Kingdom Championships, often with conspicuous success. In 1993 they won both the Horse Trials and the Showjumping Championships.

In the United States, the Pony Club was first started in 1935 by Mrs Barbara Taylor, following a visit to England. However the five branches which she succeeded in establishing in Connecticut and near Boston collapsed during the war. In 1950 Mrs Dean Bedford started a branch in Harford County, Maryland, and four years later the United States Pony Clubs, Inc., was granted a charter. Today the Pony Club is flourishing in the United States, although it is not yet as strong as it is in the United Kingdom (just over 10,000 members compared with nearly 40,000). Branches tend to be considerably smaller in numbers, with membership ranging from 25 up to 75 members, although they are likely to cover a much larger area geographically. Some branches own their own land or are able to use Hunt Club grounds.

Links between the two countries are being developed all the time: in 1992, for example, a British Tetrathlon team visited the United States and Canada and in 1993 an American Mounted Games Team visited Britain. Language difficulties do occasionally arise: rallies in the United States are competitions, whereas what are known in Britain as rallies are described on the other side of the Atlantic as mounted meetings, or, in winter, unmounted meetings or workshops. Most branches have mounted meetings weekly in the summer.

Competitions are held on a regional basis, with qualifiers going on to Nationals. Because of the distances involved, there are Western Nationals and Eastern Nationals, but every third year Nationals are held at Lexington, Kentucky and everyone from all over the country comes to these. This occasion is much looked forward to and the whole event becomes a big festival with clinics and workshops being held all week. Pony Club Headquarters were recently moved to Lexington, where many horse organisations are housed in a single building.

Mounted games in the States are open to everyone from the age of 10 right through to 21, although members of the international team were not allowed to be more than 15 on 1 January in the year in which they took part, because of the different age limits effective in Britain. The 1993 team included four girls, Mollie Strider, Krista Wilson, Robin Mason and Lorna Snook, and one boy, Charlie Conaway. They were accompanied by their trainer, Kathy Jones, with her mother, Karen Jones, as chaperone. Ten years ago Kathy was herself a member of the same team. This time they had a fascinating three weeks, with different branches of the British Pony Club hosting their visits to interesting places in Scotland, Northern England, Northern Ireland and Dublin in Eire.

The one thing which spoilt their visit was the British weather: 'It's quite nice in England, but in Scotland it just rained constantly, and the rain here, it's cold!' they complained. On the other hand, the difference in climate is partly responsible for what they see as one of the greatest disadvantages of the Pony Club in the States compared with Britain: the dearth of competitions. The only inter-branch competition available in each of the different Pony Club sports is normally the regional rally, the qualifying event for the Nationals: 'That's kind of disappointing; I wish the Pony Club had more. It's all over in one day. I think it's the weather: our summers are too hot to gallop your horse.'

Partly for this reason, the standards, at least at Regional level, are less high than in the United Kingdom. This has the advantage of offering more opportunities to the relative beginner. Robin Mason benefitted from this. She had only been in Pony Club for about a year and a half when the chance came for her to join the Games team visiting Britain. The first time she ever went to Pony Club, the Mounted Games trainer told her that they needed an extra person for the Games. 'He taught me everything in one day and we had a Rally next day and we finished up winning that and going on National and from there to the Prince Philip. It was crazy, it was really crazy. It was a freak accident.'

Other members of the team did not necessarily rate the Games as their favourite sport within the Pony Club. There was considerable enthusiasm for horse trials in particular, and, as in Britain, many of the leading international riders started off in the Pony Club. The horse trials rider David O'Connor was originally in the same branch as Kathy, Redland Hunt and Howard County, and in the showjumping world William Steinkraus is another international star who came up through the Pony Club.

Foxhunting too is widely popular, and members were only grateful that they did not suffer from the same degree of harrassment from opponents as is becoming common in Britain. Kathy described the transatlantic equivalent of the Children's Meet or Pony Club Meet. 'Each hunt has a junior hunt where the kids can come out and they pick a couple of kids each time to be staff and they go with the huntsman and the whips. All the kids foxhunt.' Younger children if they prefer can join the Hillhoppers, who simply stand on the top of the hill and watch the hunt go by. This was not enough for Robin, who recalled the excitement of one 'Juniors' Day when we got to ride right behind the huntsman and we'd just jumped this massive great coop going down a hill when the fox ran right between my pony's legs and I had to turn round and jump it back again and we only had two feet to jump it, like from a standstill.'

Members and instructors alike are unanimous in their zeal for encouraging young riders to join the Pony Club. Kathy teaches at a number of barns, or riding schools. 'Most of those kids don't have their own ponies. When they get one I say "Go to Pony Club, that's the place to go."' The members agree. 'If I had kids I'd definitely, definitely put them into Pony Club, there's no doubt about it. Just about all my friends are at Pony Club. I think it's great. I think I'd just encourage any young kid to join the Pony Club: it will teach you a lot of things which you wouldn't necessarily go out and learn on your own. Stuff like what types of feeds – I don't know many kids that are going to go out and study that on their own.'

Members are divided into many more 'ratings' than in Britain. There are tests for D, D1, D2, D3, C, C1, C2, C3, B, HA and A. As in Britain, the standard for A is extremely high. For rallies C3s, Bs and As may all be grouped together. Successes in the different tests are generally recognised at the end of the year in the Pony Club newsletter. The ratings provide a strong incentive to learn. 'In order to go up levels you have to learn. At the rallies your parents can't help you. You see a lot of kids and their parents are doing all the work for them. That's not teaching them anything, it's not teaching them how to be independent.' Working as part of a team is also important. There are teams at every level, teams for Cs, for Ds and Scrambler teams.

However the Pony Club in the States does seem to have a tendency to focus on the younger member, perhaps partly because of the problems of laying on competitions other than Regionals and Nationals for older members. 'I think it's good for beginners but in my Club there's only one B. Once you get older there are so many little kids. I think we need more older kids at least in my Club to keep it going.' This is evidently a widespread problem: 'Older kids get frustrated at rallies because we can't really do as much as we'd like, and, another thing, they pay more attention to the little kids because they need more attention. More camps and fun stuff for the little kids and not as much for the older.'

When the British Tetrathlon team, which included Julia Allen, Kate Allenby and James Whetman, visited the USA and Canada in 1992, they found that the standard at the top end was considerably lower than in Britain, with the British team conspicuously the strongest. Julia Allen felt that this was largely because of the enormous distances involved, depriving American members of the chance

The Pony Club group in Darwin, Australia 1988 after they had been droving: Peter is fifth from the right (see page 92). *(Peter Brackett)*

to practise as much as do their British counterparts by competing at numerous local events. The American National Tetrathlon team joined the British, Irish and Canadian teams in travelling round both the United States and Canada, combining matches against each other and against local branches with sight seeing. The superb organisation, for some seventy horses had to be produced on every occasion, and the welcoming friendliness of their hosts, meant that, as Julia said, 'We had some good times!'

Anyone interested in joining the Pony Club in the United States should either contact Headquarters by writing to:

United States Pony Club,
4071 Ironworks,
Lexington,
Kentucky 40511.
Telephone: 606.254.7669 Fax: 606.233.4652

or get in touch with their local District Commissioner.

Australia, with its wide open spaces and huge distances, has many of the same problems and advantages as the United States. But when Chrissy Howick of the

Axe Vale visited it, she made a different comparison. 'It is unbelievable how two organisations on opposite sides of the world can be so similar – I am referring to the Pony Clubs of England and Australia,' she wrote. Her District Commissioner, Mrs Sleight, helped her to make contact with Pony Club families in Australia, and Chrissy soon recognised the truth of the saying that people are the same the world over: 'For example, District Commissioners are generally always in a flap, always in good voice, and manage to find jobs for everyone (whether willing or not). The moment I was introduced to the District Commissioner I was an instant expert on plaiting horses in five minutes flat, dressage writing, instructing, stewarding and grooming. But the District Commissioners always produce an excellent day's entertainment which is very enjoyable for all concerned.' Parents too apparently suffer from all the same weaknesses as in England, though it is to be hoped that few mothers on either side of the world would go as far as the one whom Chrissie saw marching into the show ring with a long whip to attack pony, daughter and judge as well. Other parents were impressive in their support for the Pony Club, with a remarkable number not only attending a 'fun day' but even joining in such activities as a bareback relay. But then, even the ponies tried to help: in a 'vegetable race', whilst the rider picked up a potato to carry back before returning for further vegetables, the pony decided to save time by picking up the carrot at the same moment.

As in the States, the immense distances involved provided the main contrasts with the United Kingdom. This meant that people were prepared to drive for six or seven hours to take part in a competition. Chrissy thought the standard of riding 'slightly lower in Australia than England, but they seem to have much better prizes as a result of very interested and generous sponsors.' A benefit of the wide open spaces is that Australian Clubs have their own grounds and Club houses, which are even marked on the map. Chrissie decided this was not the extravagance it at first seemed to English eyes when she learned that 30 acres could be rented for just £5 a year.

So wherever the Pony Club flourishes, despite differences in climate and geographical conditions, in the words of Kathy Jones, 'Over all it's very similar; the same problems and the same ideals all over the world.'

— 18 —

HUNTER TRIALS

Hunter trials are the only popular form of competition in the Pony Club for which there are no qualifying Area competitions and no national Championships. Perhaps this contributes to the more relaxed atmosphere which often prevails. At hunter trials, unlike horse trials or tetrathlon, the cross-country course is not just one phase in three or four, but the sole purpose. They are usually held in spring and autumn, and in the course of the day there will be a number of different classes, usually divided according to the age of the competitor, or into novice and open classes, and those to be ridden singly, with others to be ridden in pairs. There will often be more than one course, with easier fences for Novice classes and more difficult ones for Open classes. Precise rules and definitions are left to the discretion of the branch organising the fixture.

S. John on Stacey, G. John on Pip at the Heythrop Junior Hunter Trials.
(Bob Langrish)

There are a number of other distinctions between hunter trial classes and cross-countries. Usually competitors are expected to wear correct hunting dress, that is a tweed jacket and tie, preferably a checked or spotted hunting tie, with a navy or black cap, and not cross-country colours. The course generally includes a gate to be opened and shut, and timing for this is often a decisive factor in the final result. Style of jumping too can be taken into account, particularly in pairs classes, where the object is to stay as close together as possible. The course traditionally consists of a somewhat different type of obstacle: hunter trial courses are supposed to comprise only the sort of fences likely to be met in the course of a day's hunting in the country where the event is taking place, whereas horse trials fences can be of a more complex and artificial nature. However this distinction is becoming blurred today because of the difficulties faced by most branches in finding one suitable cross-country course, much less two.

Hunter trials are fun in themselves, an excellent preparation for horse and rider for other forms of cross-country, and the novice courses are ideal for schooling young horses. Marcus and Piers Vallance, of the Bicester, who often have young ponies to school on as well as an older one to enjoy themselves with, try to go to as many hunter trials as possible. Pairs classes particularly are perfect for building up confidence in young ponies and young riders alike. Sometimes pairs consist of two members under a certain age, and sometimes of one younger and one older rider, perhaps an Associate or a parent. Many horses and ponies which refuse at every fence when competing alone on a cross-country will put in an exemplary clear round in a pair.

Like horse trials, hunter trials in the Pony Club are usually either Junior or Senior, the dividing age customarily being around 12 years. Arrangements are often made, however, for less experienced children who are technically too old to count as juniors to compete on the smaller course, either *hors concours* (HC, where they ride round but their score is not counted in the final result) or in a special novice class. Similarly, it is sometimes possible for keen younger children to compete in a senior competition.

Hunter trials are popular with riding parents: at last they too can join in. Mrs Vallance remembers 'one dad looking very solemn and I said to him 'What's the matter, James?'

'I've just been informed that this is the last year I can go as a pair with my daughter' he replied.'

19

POLOCROSSE

Polocrosse is defined as 'a team competition requiring courage, determination and all-round riding ability on the part of the rider, and careful and systematic training of the pony . . . It is suitable for ordinary children on ordinary ponies and encourages a strong and unselfish team spirit.'

The game was first introduced to the Pony Club by Mrs Genifer Malden, DC of the Ludlow branch, in 1990. Mrs Malden came from Zimbabwe, where it is extremely popular, as it is in Australia, where it was first developed before the Second World War. It is a combination of polo and lacrosse, and is a mounted team game. The object is to score goals. Each player has a special stick in which

A game in progress. *(Iain Burns)*

to catch and carry the ball. A full team is made up of six players, of whom three play at a time for an 8 minute chukka, then rest while the other three play the next chukka. This means that individual players only need one pony each, unlike polo.

Ponies which have been involved in the Prince Philip Cup or other gymkhana games show particular aptitude in learning to follow the ball, but almost any horse or pony can be taught, and a number of dressage horses are now playing. The game is proving popular with members who have excelled at Mounted Games and, on reaching 15, are no longer eligible. Many boys are particularly enthusiastic.

Polocrosse is played in three age groups, Minis who are under 12 with ponies of 13 hands and under, Juniors under 15 on ponies of 14.2 and under, and Open with no height limit.

Mrs Malden is the Pony Club Polocrosse Chairman and is doing much to help other branches to take up the sport, including arranging demonstrations by Ludlow members, and providing help with acquiring sticks.

20

TESTS

The official tests are an important aspect of the Pony Club. Despite occasional complaints, they achieve a national standard and provide a ladder for members to work their way up, a measure of achievement and an inducement to progress towards the next level. They provide a useful guideline within the branch: rides can be divided up on this basis, so that there may be rides for those working towards each of the tests. At the higher level, the tests are widely recognised by employers and colleges as providing a reliable way of assessing standards.

Sophie Allison, the National Junior Eventing Champion for 1992, is well aware of the value of passing Pony Club tests, even though it was something which at first did not come easily to her. This was partly because when younger she found it difficult to express herself sufficiently fully and clearly. Also, she says, 'I do everything my way' and it was essential to learn to do things the Pony Club way. However, she persisted with characteristic determination, and passed her C Test at the third attempt. When she later failed her H Test at the first attempt she never hesitated about retaking it, this time with success. Her sights are now set on the A Test, which she sees as much more important than the Intermediate Instructors' qualification, because so few people have it. Her mother, who failed her own A Test and has always regretted this, sees it as a really worthwhile culmination of a Pony Club upbringing to strive for and attain this ultimate accolade.

The first test which new members take is the D Test. There is no minimum or maximum age, though this is generally taken between the ages of 8 and 11. The examiner usually comes to a rally or perhaps to Junior Camp for this test. There are sections on riding, road sense and horsemastership. For riding, the member has to be able to mount and dismount, have a reasonably correct position in the saddle, know how to hold the reins and be able to ride a quiet pony safely, in an enclosed area without the leading rein, in walk and trot. Members will demonstrate this on their own, or borrowed, ponies, then be asked to do a few simple tasks like putting on the headcollar and leading the pony, and know the names of some of the points of the pony. Members who pass this test are given a yellow felt or plastic disc to wear under their Pony Club badge. This test has to be taken before members can go on to C and later tests.

Next comes the D+. This is not an essential step in the ladder, but it is a useful half way point between D and C. It is taken in similar circumstances to D, but does require a higher standard of riding and a more detailed knowledge of stable management. The recommended age is 10, and the badge colour is white.

For C Test members are usually 11 years old or more, and when they have passed the test they wear a green disc. This test is normally arranged specially, and not as part of a rally. A considerably more detailed knowledge of both riding and horsemastership is required for this test: as a guide, examiners are supposed to feel that 'the candidate would be reasonably safe, on his own, out hunting or riding in a small hunter trials.'

Before a member can pass the C Test, it is essential also to pass the Riding and Road Safety Test. This is an important and time consuming test involving detailed training, and is examined in three different phases, theory, the simulated road test with a street scene set up in a field, complete with road junctions and such hazards as people with dogs or umbrellas, and the actual road test. The complete test is either the official BHS test or a similar one laid on by the Pony Club. The next step on the ladder is, once again, an optional one: C+, with a recommended age of 14, and a pink badge. Although this test is still organised by the branch, there will usually be two examiners, both from outside the branch. Before taking C+, members must have passed C and the Riding and Road Safety test.

After this comes the challenging B Test. Here there is a mandatory minimum age of 14, and a recommended minimum age of 15 or 16. B Tests are not arranged by individual branches, but by the Area Representative, there are always at least two examiners, or more if there are more than 8 candidates, and both examiners have to be on a special list. The two examiners test the riding jointly, and this will include asking the candidates to ride each others' horses and also to ride a specially provided horse in a double bridle. There will be a variety of both show jumps and cross-country fences to jump. The examiners can then divide the stable management syllabus between them, but in the case of four candidates the stable management will last for approximately one and a half hours. For all tests, candidates should make sure that they have a copy of the card setting out the syllabus beforehand. Before signing the certificates, examiners will tell the candidates who has passed and who has failed, with some explanation. Those who have passed B Test wear a red felt.

B Test is taken by many outside authorities as indicating a reasonably high standard. For example, many Pony Club Associates are keen to spend a summer teaching riding in American summer camps. Some of the organisations require a B Test certificate as evidence of capability. Members and Associates who fail B must wait at least two months before retaking. With H and A the interval is three months. H Test is in Horsemastership only and not in riding. The minimum age is 17 and candidates must already hold B. It is the highest test of Horsemastership in the Pony Club, for A is a test of riding and of handling young and breeding stock only. H is an extremely detailed practical and theoretical exam. The felt colour is orange.

Then there is the ultimate accolade: the A Test. In 1992 just 21 people in the whole of the United Kingdom passed their A Test. The figure was the same for the previous year. One of those who passed in 1992 was Shona Riddall of the Nithsdale branch in Scotland. Shona first joined when she was a small eight-year-old. Rallies often involved a round trip of 50 miles: a long day, but perhaps this led to her mother becoming closely involved since she had always to stay for every rally: 'I showed the interest and she backed me up. Some of the kids (in the branch today) – they're showing the interest but no-one's backing them up.' Two years later Shona took her D Test. She failed. Despite this small setback, Shona was soon competing regularly in Working Hunter Pony classes and at 12 she was selected for the Inter-Branch Dressage team. A year later, she qualified individually for the Championships at Weston Park.

This dressage experience was to stand her in good stead with what Shona sees as the hardest part of the A Test. In the morning of an A Test day candidates are given rough horses to ride across-country, but in the afternoon they are required to ride Elementary Medium dressage horses. This may sound the easier task, but Shona disagrees: 'Personally I hadn't had the chance to ride enough horses schooled to that standard. It is really difficult to get that experience unless you have your own Medium Dressage horse and even if working in a dressage yard the highly schooled horses will probably be ridden by the person in charge. I had a course of lessons at Gleneagles and there I rode one horse of that standard, but ideally you need to ride about ten.'

Shona Riddall after passing her A Test.
(*Andrew McDowall, Sanquhar*)

Shona says that 'you can have plenty of experience with rough horses – go up to the local riding school and you get plenty'. Even so, it must, as she said of the Test in general, be 'very gruelling' to be expected to ride four strange horses round a cross-country course. 'You got quite good at riding your own and seeing what the other three were doing across the field, so you had an idea of what was in store.' The course used on all three occasions when Shona took her A Test was Ian Stark's schooling course. Shona found that the fences actually selected depended on the temperament of the examiners, though the candidate is not even allowed to walk the course first. It is not surprising that she comments 'Quite honestly, I don't see how anything can be as horrendous as the A Test!'

The first time she took the test, 'I was absolutely hopeless. Nerves just got to me completely. I really fluffed up in my rough riding. I was so ineffective it was unbelievable.' Next time that part went well, despite a terrible attack of nerves in the middle of the cross-country because 'it was going so well I was frightened something was going to go wrong'. Indeed, 'I came down on my schooled horses.' Irritated and exhausted, she was reluctant to accept her parents' advice to try a third time, but at least the examiners had been encouraging. For the theory questions she was glad that she had had practical experience at home of breeding and of schooling young horses. When she mounted one of the school horses after two of the other candidates had already ridden it, 'I thought "this horse is lame." So I stood up and let my reins down and it started hopping round the school.' She took it to the examiners who agreed, and she found herself riding the final horse alone, watched by everybody. At last, all was well. She was awarded the coveted blue felt badge. (The purple is reserved for those awarded Honours.)

Shona and her parents agree that the atmosphere is terrifying, particularly for candidates who have travelled an immense distance to take the test. On the occasions when Shona has taken the test, only two out of eight, or in one case three out of nine, candidates has passed. This concerned her parents, but for Shona that is part of its special attraction. 'It's so rare to meet or hear of somebody with their A Test whereas I can name you any number of Intermediate Instructors (I.I.). You can do your I.I. when you're 60, but your A Test shows that you were at that standard when you were under 21, not after 20 or 30 years' work. If you start to make it less exclusive the joy goes from it all.'

Shona is now building up her own teaching and schooling business, specialising in schooling ponies, because she is small enough. For the past two years she has trained the Nithsdale Dressage team. She is also on the Pony Club Committee, where she can represent the point of view of the members themselves, and perhaps inspire some of them to attempt to emulate her.

— 21 —

POLO

The Pony Club Polo Tournament started in 1959, only two years after the start of the Mounted Games Championship and long before the introduction of the Tetrathlon, Dressage and Showjumping Championships. But polo does seem to have enjoyed a recent surge in popularity. However, there is a marked tendency for enthusiasts to become a separate entity within their branches. Whilst the same members and associates will often be taking part in horse trials, show-jumping, dressage and tetrathlon, it is unlikely that they will also be active in polo, partly because of the different qualities required by the pony and partly because polo when taken seriously is immensely time consuming.

Only a relatively small number of branches are involved in polo. In 1992 just 35 branches entered polo teams for inter-branch competitions. Members of a branch which does not play polo can often play for a neighbouring branch. With the increasing popularity of the game, five different sections have been in-troduced dependent upon the age of the player on 1 January. There is Gannon for those under 21, Rendell for those under 18, Loriner under 16, Handley Cross under 14 and Jorrocks for those under 12.

Each division has its own rules relating to the number and type of ponies which may be used, so that younger children may only ride genuine Pony Club ponies, whereas in Gannon the game is highly competitive and professional with some Members and Associates regularly riding a number of top class polo ponies. The rules of play too are amended for the younger sections, whereas Gannon is played according to the adult Hurlingham Polo Association Rules.

A number of courses are laid on on a national basis during the Easter holidays and the early part of the summer holidays, and there is a full programme of tournaments arranged during the summer, some restricted to particular sec-tions, culminating with the Championships at Cowdray Park in the middle of August.

Charlotte Hastings belongs to the Pytchley and has been playing for some four years, since she was about eleven. 'Mum got me into it. She said one day "You're doing polo". I went along to a few practices and decided I rather liked it really. The pony is quite difficult to start off with; they don't really like it because you're not very experienced but they get more and more used to it. As the season goes on the better the pony gets.' Now her younger brother Harry is playing in the Jorrocks section and 'he really, really enjoys it because it's brilliant fun for the

The Pytchley Division 1 Loriner Team at Cowdray 1992: *(l to r)* Alex Stanhope, Charlotte Hastings, Jack Hodges, Malcolm Borwick *(behind)*, Polly Spencer, Simon Benn. *(Max Hastings)*

little ones. He scored the only goal of the season (for his team) and it gives you such a buzz: you know it's really exciting.'

Charlotte herself is now in both Rendell and Loriner and was awarded the 1993 prize for the most promising girl in the Loriner division. She has two ponies, one for each section. 'For Loriner you start having a polo pony (they look really pro and they've got these hogged manes and things) and they're usually quite old slow ones but the standard each year goes up and up. For Rendell you probably have quite a fast polo pony.' By competing in each of two sections it makes the long journeys to the matches and the stays away from home more worthwhile. For polo for those over 14 is a major commitment for the family, not only because of the pony or ponies needed but also because of the prolonged expeditions away from home necessary to take part in tournaments. Charlotte admits that 'you have to give up practically your whole summer for polo but it really is worth it.' This would be almost impossible without considerable help from the family. Charlotte's mother devotes much of her summer to providing the necessary back-up. If they do not stay away, the day can be an exhaustingly long one for players, parents and ponies alike, perhaps leaving home at six in the morning, with prize giving scheduled for 6.45 p.m. and two or three hours' driving after that. Sometimes they will stay with friends, and for the Championships at Cowdray Charlotte camps with the other competitors whilst her mother joins other parents in a nearby hotel. The season is also a longer one for the older members: Harry in Jorrocks stops around the middle of August 'because a lot of people in Jorrocks don't really take it very seriously at all, so they wander off and go on holidays whilst the rest of us are going to the Championships.'

Chances of reaching the Championships in polo are considerably higher than in any other discipline in the Pony Club. In Loriner for example, in 1993, 18 out of 22 teams qualified. The relatively small number of people involved and the fact that most competitions are arranged on a national rather than a local basis contributes to the special atmosphere of the Pony Club polo world. Charlotte feels that 'there are pros and cons of having so many people around you. You do get slightly tired of them before the end of the season, but it's also really nice to see all your friends on every day of the holidays practically, and to meet lots more people.' There are also scholarship schemes establishing links between young players in this country and their South American counterparts. In 1993 a group of five Chileans visited this country. One of them stayed at Charlotte's home, and they had a barbecue for all the host families. Should Charlotte ever take up her invitation to visit Chile, however, she will occasion some surprise, for Chilean girls are not allowed to play. One English girl who travelled out on a polo scholarship found that her hosts had never seen a girl play before. When the game started, nobody marked her at all and she had scored a considerable number of goals unopposed before her opponents realised what was happening.

The skills required for polo are different from those needed for other forms of riding. Whilst controlling the pony accurately and spontaneously is essential, the best polo players are always good games players, with an eye for a ball and the ability to play in a team. Regular practice together is essential. Pytchley members are fortunate in having a polo ground at Newnham where they can have practice chukkas. The teams are masterminded by Luke Borwick, who is also responsible for the Handley Cross section for the whole of Britain. His son Malcolm is one of the outstanding young players in the Pony Club today. The popularity of polo has drawbacks for the branch: whilst several of the polo playing members hunt in winter, few have time for other Pony Club activities in summer. New recruits are lent polo sticks when they first start playing, though they are expected to provide their own (a further expense, as sticks are easily broken) if they wish to play regularly.

Whilst her mother sometimes finds the game somewhat unnerving, even as a spectator, following an accident when the ball hit her hard on the foot, Charlotte is less concerned. 'From the spectator's point of view it seems more scary than you actually feel in the chukka. But a lot of people can get pretty vicious. People can also get really hyped up and start shouting all the time. When you are ridden off it is painful.' Charlotte ensures that she always wears her knee pads ever since an episode when her knees were cut and bleeding following a ride off. Whilst at Jorrocks level this is unnecessary and members just wear ordinary riding hats, older players wear polo helmets, and face masks are optional. Ponies' legs are always protected with boots or bandages. Much of the attraction of the game, for spectators and players alike, was summed up by Charlotte when she said 'It's all speed and everything hangs on a thread'.

There are complicated rules relating to handicapping in Pony Club polo, which are different from those in the adult game. But perhaps after all the position was best summed up by a member of a branch where polo is not played. She was asked in a quiz what the handicap was for a beginner at polo, and replied 'Not being able to hit the ball?'

ASSOCIATES

There is no minimum age for joining the Pony Club, but membership finishes on 1 January after a member's 18th birthday. On that date, the Member becomes an Associate. For three more years, until 1 January in the year following their 21st birthday, they may continue to take a full part in all Pony Club activities, apart from the rules, different for each discipline, concerning eligibility for Inter-Branch teams. In many branches, Associates form their own group or Junior Committee, holding meetings and laying on functions for younger members of the branch, to raise funds or for their own entertainment.

Jo Lister and Emma Young, who are both 18, run the Associates Club for the West Hampshire, helped by a third friend who has less time as she is working. Jo and Emma are old friends: they started riding together at a riding school when they were 14. 'I was just working for rides there really, and we were always saying "We've got to get away and do something." We didn't know anything about Pony Club or that you didn't have to have your own pony. I cannot believe what I would be doing if I hadn't started going, to be honest, because I don't really like doing anything else. All the friends I've made as well. It's quite amazing looking at it like that. I'd probably be doing an office job or something.'

Emma is in fact a working pupil at a driving yard whilst Jo is still at college completing her A levels. When they first joined, neither girl had a pony of her own, though they did each get one soon after. Jo shared hers with her younger sister so had to borrow one for camp. Emma remembers her first rally: 'I had one of the riding school ponies and I'd never jumped in my life before. I was a bit embarrassed to say so and I think I got put in the wrong group. I was jumping the quarry on the open course and when we came down to the bottom of the hill the pony went left and I went right and there was a tree in between.'

Soon they were taking part in everything through the Pony Club, dressage, showjumping including the Area team, hunting, camp and taking tests: both hold their B Test and are working for H, and for Emma this has helped enormously with her BHS exams. Jo is modest about her horse and herself: 'We dabble in everything and don't do very well but we have fun.' Now that they are Associates, they have both been doing some teaching and Jo also 'nannies' at camp.

Their Associates Club organises carol singing at Christmas. 'We went round about eleven pubs and raised £150 for the Riding for the Disabled Fortune

Centre. It was really good fun. We had about 20 children and said "Don't worry if you can't sing."' They also arrange rallies, trying to make them more interesting for the younger ones, are thinking of starting polocrosse and run a Christmas disco. 'We try to organise fun events for the younger ones so there's time for others to organise stuff for us!'

Jo and Emma do their best to ensure that younger members have all the opportunities they would have liked themselves. Their only regret is not joining the Pony Club younger: 'If I had been in the Pony Club at a younger age I probably would have done a lot more competitive riding. I would say definitely go out and join straight away, don't even wait until you've learnt to ride (even without a pony of your own). You're going to make friends with the people who have the ponies. My riding improved so quickly just by being with people who ride better. There's one boy who is on a different pony at every rally because people are lending him ponies and he's gone from not having ridden to C+ standard in a year. Incredible, but it just shows it can be done.'

In the Staff College and Sandhurst branch, the Chairman of the Junior Committee is 19-year-old Malcolm Clapson. As a small boy he at first showed little enthusiasm for riding, but the family had an adored coloured pony called Splash, whose previous owners had bought him off the meat wagon at Guildford market ('he was a very tubby skewbald: he would have made a lot for meat'). Malcolm's sister had outgrown Splash and, his mother says, 'We made him ride because we never ever wanted to sell the pony!' Splash, now in his thirties, is still doing tetrathlons with a 'mini' in the branch and still belongs to the Clapson family. According to Malcolm, they were noticed soon afterwards: 'My goodness, that pony's good. Can the boy swim or run?' and thus his career in the tetrathlon was launched. In 1989 he was one of the team which won the Boys' Tetrathlon Championships.

Tetrathlon suits Malcolm perfectly for he loves the cross-country. 'I think it's the thrill of it, and I'm a lot more competent at cross-country than I am at showjumping.' He enjoys horse trials too, and says 'I think the jumps in Tet are a lot larger and a lot more frightening than in horse trials. To be perfectly honest with you I hate doing flat work – I think its the most boring thing – Typical boy! Jack (his horse) does an excellent dressage test but I'm afraid the rider's not very competent with the aids!'

But Malcolm is an excellent team member and as he is in the horse trials team he has been working on this because 'I don't really want to let anybody down.' When competing as an individual, his mother complains that 'he doesn't care if he wins or loses!' In a recent horse trial 'I thought I'd gone clear, but I'd actually missed out a jump! I would have been fourth.' He laughs but his mother thinks 'boys are very frustrating. We used to tell the pony which fences to jump because there was no point in telling Malcolm. His sister was always so much more organised.'

Malcolm Clapson at Area Horse Trials at Iping 1991 on Jack.
(Paul Saville, Pleasure Prints)

Malcolm considers that 'the greatest thing about the Pony Club is the ability to make relationships not only with other people but with your horse as well', and he and Jack do have an exceptional relationship. Jack has tremendous personality, and he and his rider play games in the field, chasing each other in fun, in a manner more human than equine. At weekends, Malcolm likes 'to go out with Jack and put my back pack on and take a flask and some sandwiches.' Sometimes they meet up with friends, often they ride for miles alone.

For the rest of the week, like so many Pony Club members, life is always full. He is up at half past six to feed and exercise Jack, and after college he fits in two evenings' work, two swims and a shooting session, not to mention his love for amateur dramatics and all the time he devotes to the Junior Committee. 'I think the worst thing about horses is having to clean tack. I just hate it so much, so I get my mum to do it for me now!'

He considers that the important thing with the Junior Committee was to win the confidence of the parents, so started with a skittles evening with a barbecue and music to which about 100 parents came. 'They won't let you take the kids off their hands unless they trust you, but we put on something that seemed to be well run and well organised and I think they liked that.' Since then his Committee has laid on a number of parties, including a ball at Ascot held jointly with the Garth. These have proved more popular, and indeed more profitable, than visits to 'horsey places. I think the kids are so orientated to horses anyway that they need a break.' They also organise one evening's entertainment during camp, have a barbecue with a bouncy castle, a popular treasure hunt (in cars with parents) and organise a group to paint show jumps in the autumn.

Malcolm has been in his Inter-Branch team for showjumping and horse trials as well as the tetrathlon, where the team were runners-up at the Championships for several years before their eventual victory in 1989. In one particularly memorable year, the Area Showjumping was in the Isle of Wight, where the wonderfully hospitable branch arranged for every competitor in addition to over 100 horses to be put up with different families, and all were invited to a barbecue. Malcolm thought this 'absolutely terrific,' though he does not remember his own performance in the showjumping with such enthusiasm: 'They said to me when I get to this last jump "For goodness' sake pull him back, it's down hill". What did I do? I got all the way round and I thought "Clear round; let him go", and he knocked it down.'

With all his activities and irresistible sense of humour, it is hardly surprising that he recently won the cup for the most outstanding member or associate. Branches with Junior Committees such as these are fortunate indeed.

A DREAM COME TRUE

Sarah Rice dreamed of riding her own pony across the moor. For Thomas Berry the dream was of fun, jokes and laughter with his friends whilst working towards a career with horses. Karen Wheatley, born profoundly deaf in London's Docklands, dreamed of learning to ride properly. Shona Riddall yearned to achieve the highest accolade open to a young rider by passing her A Test. Camilla Hall dreamed of tranforming a farmer's driving pony into a top dressage performer and Sophie Allison of becoming a champion in the world of three-day eventing. Marion Nairn dreamed of captaining the winning team in the Prince Philip Cup at Wembley.

Camilla Fraser dreamed of riding in beautiful country with her friends, and Jo Lister of being part of a group who shared her love of horses. Louisa Myatt longed to compete as a member of a successful team whilst for Pippa Langston the dream was of riding on equal terms with others despite her health, and helping the younger members. Julia Allen, Kate Allenby and Natalie Gerard dreamed of the challenge of competing in four sports simultaneously, and Chrissy Howick of seeing other countries. Mark Colvin sought a career in a field where he excelled, and Peter Brackett craved the excitement of crossing the world. Mary Thomson dreamed of winning Badminton, of riding in the Olympics. All of them, and so many more, have been helped to realise their dreams by the Pony Club.

If horses and ponies feature in your dreams, and you are under 21, come and join us. Membership costs just £19.50 a year, with a one-off joining fee of £1 (1994 rates). Write or telephone your local District Commissioner or Secretary, or, if you do not know where to find them, write first to:

The Pony Club,
The British Equestrian Centre,
Stoneleigh Park,
Kenilworth,
Warwickshire CV8 2LR

and they will give you all the information you need.

INDEX